$6.00

BRANCHES ON THE CONEJO

Leaving the Soil after Five Generations

To Katie,
enjoy my tale
of the Conejo -
Anne Schroeder

Anne Schroeder

Branches on the Conejo
by
Anne Schroeder

First Edition : November, 2001

ISBN 1-891954-99-7

Library of Congress Cataloging-in-Publication Data.

Library of Congress Control Number: 2001118566

Schroeder, Anne: (1948-   )
Branches on the Conejo/Anne Schroeder   p.cm.—
(Russell Dean and Company—non-fiction)

1. History (California). 2. Non-Fiction. I. Title. II. Series

Russell Dean books are printed on acid-free paper, and meet the guidelines for permanence and durability of the Committee on Production Guidelines for Book Longevity of the Council on Library Resources.

All Rights Reserved. Dust jacket design by Betula Productions, Atascadero, California. All photographs used with permission.

Printed in the United States of America.

RUSSELL DEAN and COMPANY, Publishers
Santa Margarita, California U.S.A.

DEDICATION

This book is dedicated to the Spirit of the Pioneer.
May it live and prosper inside us all.

ACKNOWLEDGMENTS

I am deeply indebted to a number of people for sharing their memories, for pointing me correct, for opening their family albums and their memories. This book could not have been written without the help of many family members who contributed their stories. This is truly a collective oral history set into print.

First and foremost, thanks are due to my aunt and our family historian, Mary Olsen Rydberg, who spent years gathering information from public sources and family members. Mary is a child of the Conejo Valley; her albums include information on every member of the Borchard/Kelley/Olsen families. Without her accurate documentation, this project would not have been possible. Mary recorded many of the stories that I used from the memories of her aunt, Babe Kelley.

My mother, Eugenia (Jean) Olsen Thompson, now the oldest living family member, spent many days recalling stories that would have been lost otherwise. She provided both tone and reason to my search for our family identity.

Cousin Fred Kelley corresponded via e-mail and gave a balanced view to the Kelley history. Uncle Neil Olsen recalled the postwar era. Cousin Jerry Olsen verified the history of the Norwegian Colony and provided technical advice and his own well-documented research papers. Dwayne Dotson recalled the cowboy days of the Conejo.

Others who provided direction and encouragement include: The Honorable William Clark and his cousin, Patricia Clark Doerner, Charles Johnson and Tim Schiffer of the Ventura County Historical Museum, Sandy Hildebrandt of the Stagecoach Inn Museum. I am indebted to the Scandinavian American Cultural and Historical Foundation for sponsoring my work.

My husband, Steve Schroeder, deserves special thanks for his unwavering support. He believes in me.

Branches on the Conejo

TABLE OF CONTENTS

PROLOGUE

In the months following Nana's passing, I eased the pain in my empty heart by thinking about her life. So clearly did I recall the events of our time together that I began to write them in my journal. Often in dreams she visits.

She was not always "Nana". I began using the name in my writing after she died. Before that she was simply "Grandma", but afterwards I needed something of her for my own. Her grandchildren numbered twenty-six; what right did I have—did anyone have—to speak for her? "Nana" belonged in my memories.

Fourteen years after her passing, I am still haunted by her loss. We were blessed with a long and close relationship. Why then did her death at 86 leave me so bereft? Why, fourteen years later, am I still grieving? It was in the course of writing that I came to realize the roots of my sorrow. I grieve for my grandmother, of course, but in a larger sense I mourn the loss of an era, of innocence, of all that was and can no longer be; a time when life unfolded with such freshness and wonder that it molded my psyche.

My grandparents lived in a world where events passed in slow, measured cadence. They were predictable, comfortable people whose lives evolved slowly enough that twenty grandchildren shared the same experiences: orange sherbet served in carnival glass bowls on Friday evenings; television with only one channel; the feel and scent of starched sheets on the guest bed; the smell and sound of an air-tight DeSoto sedan—the stuff of memories.

For me, what disappeared with Nana's passing represents the very best of rural America. Nana stood as an icon to practicality, perseverance and grit. She saw her duty, and she fulfilled it clearly and simply.

Grandpa was a Renaissance man, a free thinker. Fiercely pragmatic, steadfast in his beliefs, he was a man whose lifetime spanned the apex of American farming. Only once did he leave his farm, to spend two weeks on a jury for a murder trial in Ventura. He was a trustee for the school board, a civil servant, a man whose farm implements and family photographs are displayed in the Stagecoach Inn Museum in Newbury Park, the heart of his beloved Conejo (cone-ay-ho, Spanish for "rabbit").

He was a talented machinist, a man who lived his belief in the dignity of all men. We, his progeny, have cause to be proud of the Norwegian blood that courses through our veins. Ours is the practical, hard-working legacy of plain-faced European immigrants who built America, and their own futures, one dollar at a time.

Is it any wonder that when I recall Nana and Grandpa, my body relaxes and my mind escapes to a quieter, gentler time?

BRANCHES ON THE CONEJO

Leaving the Soil after Five Generations

Anne Schroeder

Anne Schroeder

Chapter One
Sweet Partings

In her final days, the trees that Nana planted as a new bride stood her vigil in the early morning while the first buds of the cottonwood brushed against the naked windowsill. The wind became her ally in the way that it scraped and worried the brittle winter branches against the lapboard siding of the farmhouse. No longer an annoyance, the harsh energy of the northeast winds gave voice to the anger that raged within her. She spoke of none of this, but I saw her eyes glisten as she fought to control the last vestiges of her destiny. She was my mother's mother, Theresa Kelley Olsen. Nana.

I am her namesake. I learned her ways in unspoken parody, shared her thoughts over innumerable mugs of milk-tea and cookies. In the last days, I saw the torment that clouded her gray eyes.

As she lay dying, it was the trees that captured her essence, the ancient elms and cottonwoods that shattered the stark sunlight into a canopy of lace, a whisper of light upon raging conflict.

In her last days she wavered between consciousness and respite. Watching her, I learned that death is summoned when the will to live grows weary. When Nana's fierce hold on life ebbed, her mind accepted eternity as her destiny. She did not invite death into herself as much as she allowed life to leave.

With her other grandchildren, I took turns spelling our mothers and aunts at Nana's bedside, my sense of place akin to holding a second trust deed on a house about to be repossessed. The older generation held the first claim. They relayed the doctor's information to the rest of us and we waited to be told the news. Our family is not one to store its mourning clothes in the back closet. We showed our respect up front and personal, in the weeks and days when waiting by her bedside was all that we could do.

When the time came for final good-byes, I found myself unable to face the task alone. Nana lay so still, so pliant, little more than a pile of bedclothes arranged against a blue waffle-weave blanket. A plastic chair stood at the foot of her bed but I ignored it. I had not made my journey to sit so far from her side.

I shared my visit with a brother and a cousin, quiet farmers who masked their grief in mute misery and hung back while their sadness crowded the room. My throat choked with the rawness of farewell. My reason for coming had been simple; I thought that I could bear to let her go if I could only hold her hand once more. I leaned close and whispered while I stroked her fingers, brushed them against my cheek. I felt her pulse, so faint, so patient, as though she was waiting for each of us to say goodbye. *What must she be thinking?* I wondered. *What must she be thinking?*

As though she read my thoughts, Nana opened her eyes, her weary smile conveying surprise that we had come.

I felt blessed to find her awake, had been warned to expect otherwise. Seeing her so still, so helpless, seemed to punch the air from my diaphragm. When I could breathe again, loneliness filled the space in my lungs. She wasn't even gone, and already I felt the bleakness of her loss.

I swallowed the lump in my throat and returned her smile. She seemed to be waiting to speak. I made up my mind not to tire her, but the words slipped out, one by one. Like old times we chatted, the two of us, alone almost. Her mind remained keen to the last. Leaning into the bed, I reminded her of the lessons that she had taught us, named a dozen trips we had shared, reminisced of summers at her beachhouse. Had my mother been present she would have thought our conversation odd. She might have cautioned me not to tire Nana. My words continued, weighed against the need in Nana's eyes.

Never one to suffer tears, that day Nana fretted for her judgment, for the time when God would tally the product of her life. "It doesn't hurt now," she said. "I just make a lot of noise." So undignified, these words on a deathbed, that we both laughed.

I smiled at her words, turned to see the graven faces of the men behind me, imagined their throats with lumps they could not swallow. A spokes-grandchild, I wanted to say something for each of us. "You've taught us how to live, now you're showing us how to die."

"I hope so." With the quiet words she ceased fidgeting her arthritic fingers on the chenille bedspread and turned her face towards me. For long seconds we studied each other. In the silence we said all that needed saying while eternity waited behind the wisdom of her eyes. I held her gaze and prayed that Heaven would be the place where we would next meet.

I read in her eyes a sudden flash of panic that betrayed a fear too strong to dismiss. Such blasphemy to a dying soul would be the greatest sin of all. In silence, I promised that I would pray for her, would hold her close for all the days that separated us. I repeated the promise softly so she could hear it.

This seemed to be what she sought. The storm left her eyes and serenity surrounded her like a mantle.

I wanted to weep for what I had stolen from my brother, my cousin, what I had seen in the depths of Nana's eyes while they waited at the door. I wanted them to step closer, to hold her hand, to smooth her brow and feel the softness of her skin, but the distance from the door to her bedside was a journey that neither could take. *How terrible to be a man,* I thought, *that their tears should be choked behind their sadness.*

Ashen-faced, it was all they could do to lean against the wall and cast long glances at the floor. Their scattered gaze didn't rest long on Nana. I thought again of how good it was to be a woman, to let tears stream down my face and to let my words quiver when I couldn't finish a sentence. Never have I loved either of them more, my brother or my cousin, than on that day. Never have I loved Nana more.

Nana's daughters arrived from their coffee. "She didn't speak, did she? She's been in a coma for three days," my mother whispered.

I glanced at the farmers, but they made my decision no easier. They left it to me whether I should lie, to decide whether my truth would be too cruel. Turning back, I saw that Nana had slipped into her peaceful place. She did not speak again.

I found it hard to think that Nana would hide from her daughters on her deathbed, but such are the secrets that temper our lives. Perhaps I, too, will hide from my children when they confer with the doctor over my bedside and fret about whether the room is too warm. Nana would have said that such issues between mother and daughter are understandable.

Sometimes children are a responsibility that arrives when we, as women, are trying to find our own fit in the fabric of life. It was so with my mother. It is so with my own children. As her granddaughter, I remained unaware of the fractures in her relationships. Her children undoubtedly thought otherwise, but to me

Nana never seemed to make a misstep.

Fortune graced her with the perfect place to grow up, the Conejo Valley of Southern California during its last vestige of rural seclusion. Fortune graced her with a birth in a centennial year, 1900, and with a twin brother, John Louis. The fact that she was born in Talbert, California was merely an accident of necessity. Her parents, Rosa and Silas Kelley were farming the flatlands near Huntington Beach when Nana was born, November 19, 1900, during the 100-year flood. That same flood cut short her father's farming venture and washed his topsoil into the Pacific Ocean.

Eventually, they returned to the Conejo. Rosa and her babies waited out the winter until the rains and the winds ceased. By April, the adobe wagon ruts had dried to a passable sludge. Nana and her twin were five months old and their brother Charlie, two years, when Rosa loaded them into a wagon and drove the buckboard single-handedly through the badlands of Calabasas. Silas rode with them to the Ventura County line to protect them from highwaymen, then turned back, alone.

Rosa returned home to the Conejo, arranged for the baptisms of her babies and never left again. When his summer crops were harvested, Silas returned as well.

Two more sons were born, one fifteen months after the other, so that Rosa had five children under the age of seven. It was some years before three other daughters were born. Genetically, the blend of Irish with German proved to be a good match; all the babies lived.

Nana grew up with four feisty brothers who teased her unmercifully and wore their mother out trying to keep them safe and occupied. Left with only boys for company, Nana learned to drive a buggy, to saddle her horse and to ride with a man's ease.

The tempo of her life maintained an assurance that there would be time for everything that she wanted to do. The grain-

Nana at age 12 sat a horse with a man's ease. 1912.

fields outside her father's door provided a rhythm that varied only with the seasons. In later years, Nana planted trees with the certitude that she would still be living in the same house when they matured.

I was fortunate to experience the 1950s, the last decade of simplicity, and to have Nana as a mentor. She taught me lessons that have served me well: during a woman's youth, if she is lucky, she learns who she is not. During the early decades of adulthood, she strives to become the person that she wants to be. By the time she reaches fifty, she should be embracing life's possibilities. By the time grandchildren arrive, a woman should be nothing less than what her destiny requires. A woman should live her life so that her grandchildren will learn from her. These are the lessons that Nana taught me. When I have grandchildren I shall teach them the same.

I was thirty-eight the year that Nana died, old and young at the same time. My daughter was eighteen. I looked at her and thought how young she was, devoid of wisdom over things that matter in life, such as glimpsing death waiting behind clouded eyes.

When our matriarch passed away, adjustments rippled throughout the bloodline. Daughter took mother's place, mother became grandmother and sister became aunt. Lives took on mortal imperative. Memories were revisited, formed, categorized and saved in the places that remained. With Nana's passing, new vitality flowed into the waiting rootstock, new branches separated from old trunks.

Strange, the things that I missed with the death of a grandmother, the things that I connected with her in the hope that life could be the same again. Often, the things that one wants to claim as keepsake would make no sense to anyone else.

My childhood memories were embedded in an old clock that I found sitting on her nightstand on the day of her funeral. The alarm on Nana's Big Ben clock no longer rang, nor did the hands move when I picked it up carefully, the way she showed me as a child. For years it sat on her night table, cosied up against flattened tubes of Ben Gay and her coil of rosary beads. I used to play with it, fit its brass key into the four-sided stem and wind it clockwise until it was too hard to turn. "Don't overwind," she would warn.

Her words seemed to link us as I sat on her double bed and tried to remember the way that things used to be. Long ago, when the clock had ticked, I'd watch to see if the key turned, but it was like trying to watch the moon advancing across the sky, always too gradual for the eye to see.

Settings could be adjusted on the back of the clock with tiny brass fittings marked with capitol letters "Loud" and "Soft". I used to set off the alarm by jangling the twin domes with my finger while Nana tidied up, vacuuming the floor with her Electrolux. The last time I wound it, the clock stopped working. Nana said it probably wore out just like her vacuum cleaner, its flannel bag mended repeatedly on her ancient Singer sewing machine, its frayed cord covered with black electrical tape. Nana used a tool for as long as it served its purpose. Someone got her a radio alarm clock for Christmas but she left the old one on her night table.

The night of her funeral, I slipped into her room, played with the key, held the clock up to my ear and tried to coax a *tick* from its worn-out innards. I thought about slipping it into my pocket, but that would nullify the trust that our family held in each other. I rested my face on her pillow, smelled her talc and liniment. For a minute she was still there and I was a child, playing with the clock.

Nana's funeral was celebrated with jubilation; she had gone to be with her Father. The Mass was held in Oxnard's Santa Clara Church, with its beautiful domed ceilings and frescos nearly as old as Nana herself. The church exuded a serenity that belonged to another time. I arrived early for the service, wearing a light-colored dress because I refused to wear black for Nana. Alone in the quiet church, I allowed my mind to associate events of her life. She would have enjoyed the setting. She would have agreed that a church is the only place to hold a funeral, especially a small, domed church like Santa Clara that smelled of beeswax and musty wood when the door was first opened.

Her funeral did not provide the solace I sought. I waited for a feeling of letting go, of saying good-bye, that never came. The eulogy, given by a priest who never knew Nana, skimmed the highpoints of her life without touching her essence, like a book reviewed by someone who had only seen the movie.

Nana had issues with the Roman Catholic Church, issues more to do with practicality than matters of faith. She lived in an era when, in order to take Communion on Sunday, the faithful were obliged to attend Saturday Confession. In the middle of the day, when the garden needed harvesting and she was steamy from canning, she would tussle with her spiritual conscience. If she did not travel the eight miles to attend four o'clock Confession, she was sure to regret it at Mass the next morning. Sometimes she made the trip, sometimes not. If any priest had cared to visit, she believed that he would clearly see that a farmwife's daily chores were penance enough for any sins she might have committed.

As a child I attended funerals for Nana's aunts and uncles, ancient men and women whose children and grandchildren filled several rows in St. Mary Magdalen's Catholic Church in Camarillo where we all worshipped each Sunday. The names of Nana's aunts and uncles, the Borchards, were as familiar to me as the Yankees might be to a group of children playing stickball in the streets of New York. I knew them all, viewed them in their caskets with their cheeks painted the false blush of death.

I attended funerals with a sense of the natural order of life's cycle, six before I reached my twelfth birthday, as many again in the next decade. Death left its indelible impression. I learned that the only lasting virtue lies in living a practical, frugal, hardworking life.

The family followed the deathbed progress of each great-great aunt and uncle. Funerals were highly anticipated events with elegant caskets, incense, old-fashioned flowers propagated and grown from seeds in home gardens. Nana's aunts and uncles were wealthy people. Their funerals were significant affairs. Surviving sisters and brothers would arrive in chauffeur-driven limousines, dressed in the same clothing that they wore to church on Sundays. They did not buy new outfits to bury their dead.

Hothouse carnations and roses surrounded Nana's casket, but it was her Brazilian pepper tree that filled my senses, the peace of her farmhouse evenings that I revisited while the church filled up behind me. Brazilian pepper trees will always be Nana to me.

In the church, the priest blessed the casket and sprinkled it with holy water. He returned to the altar, retrieved a smoking incense burner suspended from a long, silver chain and rocked it from side to side, spilling incense into the room. Closing my eyes, I felt languor steal through me. I recalled when, long ago, I sat next to Nana, who dressed like the Queen Mother in her white gloves and stiff black hat, and tried not to twitch when the service ran long.

Chapter Two
Nana's House

Whenever my mother allowed me to spend the weekend at Nana's, the experience seemed sweeter than Heaven. Once every two weeks my mother, brother and two sisters and I made the seven-mile trip to Nana's and Grandpa's, a twenty-minute drive over sloping knolls onto Olsen Road, named for my grandfather's family.

While my mother and Nana visited, we were free to explore. All afternoon we searched the woodlands and followed the creek as far as the barbed-wire fence at the Janss Ranch. We climbed the hayloft, rode the pulley ropes to the ground and frightened the penned sheep. Once, we climbed the rickety ladder to stare at a sleeping barn owl and nearly got ourselves clawed for our efforts.

When Nana and my mother strolled toward our beige Studebaker, Nana with a bouquet of newspaper-wrapped hollyhocks or irises, it was time to leave. If it was Friday, and if Nana was planning to attend our church on Sunday, one of us got to spend the night. Usually it was I who would stand beside Nana while my mother drove off, my heart beating to the rhythm of my thoughts; *my turn...my turn.*

As soon as the Studebaker rounded the curve, Nana was mine. But there were rules to be obeyed. We waved my family off and returned to the house. I washed hands and face and set the table with an efficiency that would have surprised my mother.

Supper meant chicken soup with thick homemade noodles, plain soda crackers with store-bought butter. Knudsen cottage cheese came straight from a yellow and white carton. It tasted sweet and creamy compared to my mother's homemade. Nana served it with canned cling peaches spooned from a quart Mason jar.

Evenings were tranquil; the routine varied little over fourteen years. Grandpa would scan the *National Geographic* or *Farm Journal* while Nana read the newspaper, delivered by carrier in the late afternoon. At seven o'clock, I'd dish orange sherbet into three carnival-glass dishes, careful that each contained exactly the same amount. With my stocking feet tucked beneath me, I'd sit in a Queen Anne leather chair and nibble mouse bites of sherbet while a hearth fire crackled behind us.

It was always Nana's house, even though Grandpa built it before their marriage. They completed it together in the two weeks following their wedding in 1921, while living in Moorpark with Grandpa's parents, Nils and Ellen Olsen.

The house was ship-lap, a single-story farmhouse, designed with hidden crannies. In the living room, a storage bench spanned two china cabinets. A window-less window-seat, its dark wood accenting intricate, hand-forged metal pulls, housed an antique Norwegian fiddle and a wooden flute. At the end of the hall stood an ancient-looking pump organ, a second-hand survivor of a 1930s voyage from Germany. Cherrywood cabinets lined one wall of the narrow dining room, their shelves filled with silver, crystal and china dishes. Some dishes were dime-store pretties, others had been brought over from the "old country". All were precious because of post-war scarcity.

Down the hall, between the living room and Nana's bedroom, was her guestroom. Its luxurious double bed, mounded with a white chenille bedspread and starched pillowcases, filled the room. Nana required that her younger guests take a bath every night before bed so that the sheets could be used for the next grandchild.

As a five-year-old, I'd dally until Nana's bedtime warning turned hard-edged and I knew that she meant it. Nana wasn't the tucking-in sort of grandmother, but the bid-you-goodnight-in-the-living-room type. I had to make the dark trek down the hall by myself. Pausing at the door, I'd gulp air, hit the light switch and make a flying leap into bed. I would hide motionless under the covers until my pulse slowed, my eyelids grew heavy and I slept.

During the night the peacocks called from high in the willow trees. The homely little guinea hens issued rude squawks. Coyotes howled from the Indian caves at the top of the bluff. Sometimes the hound dog that slept beneath my window snarled low in its throat and tore off down the path after a rabbit or fox. Nana thought I was an easy sleeper because the bed was scarcely rumpled in the morning. Had I told her about my night terrors she would have decided that I was too young to stay alone.

Like Nana's house itself, every item held a permanence that I failed to recognize at the time. Plastic was just making its appearance. Nana's things were crafted of hardwood or leather, brass or thick glass. Grandpa's paperweights, his magnifying glass, his fountain pens and ink jars were meant to last several lifetimes.

In the manner of a woman who appreciated her belongings and the labor it had taken to earn them, Nana kept a spotless house and filled it with only those items that served a purpose. Her leather chairs and ottoman had a weathered comfort born of hard use. Her carpets were area rugs, purchased at the time of her marriage. Her furniture smelled of lemon polish. She kept vases filled with fresh flowers from her garden for as long as she was able to grow them.

Her house came alive when visitors arrived. During the winters, the hearth held a smoldering log day and night. In the center of her kitchen table she kept an ancient canister filled with cookies, home-baked for most of her life, store-bought when arthritis inflamed her joints and twisted her fingers. Everyone who passed through her kitchen knew they could help themselves to her larder. She kept a trio of favorite teapots, their faded gold rims and nicks familiar to everyone who ever sat her table.

Her parents were coffee drinkers. After her marriage, she and Grandpa could not afford to buy both tea and coffee. She switched to tea like the other Norwegians.

At tea time, Grandpa would come in from the fields to snack on tea and a cold pancake from the breadbox, topped with a thin layer of jam. Sometimes neighbors would drop by to share stories and laugh. Those were the times that I loved the best.

Memories of Nana invariably involved some sort of task. She lived in the here-and-now, brusquely intent on keeping idle hands occupied. She was not an easy taskmaster, not prone to compliments or easy assurances, never a hugger or a woman given to praise. Her sharpness was not to be taken personally; it was just her way—and that of her mother. I am not alone in my feelings. All of her grandchildren learned that the absence of criticism was proof of a job well done. We were raised with an obligation to keep up Nana's house and her yard, and I never doubted her right to my labors.

By eight years of age we were expected to wield a hoe in the flowerbeds without chopping a seedling. We were expected to distinguish pickled beets on the canning shelf from crabapples, quart from pint, to fetch last year's remains before starting on the new. "Put it on the counter," meant that we had plucked the right jar.

We learned that a warning was given only once. Mistakes held consequence: a bee sting for forgetting to wear shoes when we hung laundry, rattlesnakes in the flowerbeds if we didn't keep watch, no lunch until chores were finished. Nana's reward came in the way that she shared her world.

In later years this economy of praise became a common family trait. Caught between the New Education, with its happy faces, gold stars and praise—however slightly earned—some of us felt pressure to assume a style that did not sit well with our basic tenets. In those days, a job done well was its own reward. A child should act in a given manner because it was the right thing to do. Nana was stingy with her praise, probably because she had never known any other way.

One of the rooms in Nana's house was inviolate: Uncle Neil's bedroom, empty because he was off at high school and later, college. As rooms went, it was tiny and spare, with a desk, a single bed, a closet. His bookshelves held a treasure-trove of adventures, thirty-five cent westerns with paperback covers, most of them featuring heroes in high noon shootouts.

One afternoon I slipped into his room and found a paperback with a picture of Red Ryder, rugged and lean-jawed, relaxing after a day of grueling western adventure. Behind him, a window—amazingly similar to those in Nana's guestroom—opened onto the night sky. Crouched at the edge of the sill, ready to leap upon the unsuspecting Red Ryder was a cougar, its face distorted in a feral scream that silenced the wind.

Time and again I sneaked into the room to study that book. I searched the pages of indecipherable print for some hint of Red Ryder's fate. My older brother, seven and scarcely reading, wasn't much help. We studied the picture together and agreed that, surely, things looked grim for Red. There was no one that I could ask. Nana would have told me to shut the door and get away. My writer's imagination was born in that room, inventing scenarios to rescue Red Ryder from certain death.

Grandpa's barnyard formed an elliptical corral of outbuildings constructed by the combined efforts of Norwegian carpenters. Electricity had come to the farm in 1935 and the power room that had once housed the gasoline-powered generator was no longer needed so we used it as a playroom. An electric pump pushed water up to the tank house and then into the house. The machine shop had the unmistakable odor of spilled diesel fuel on its powdery dirt floor. With its honey processing room, aviary, and hen house, the row of outbuildings made the yard resemble Main Street on a western movie set.

In 1947, phone lines were extended from Peder Pederson's house on Moorpark Road to Grandpa's front yard at a cost of $154 plus the expense of the telephone poles. The cost was divided between the four families of the Norwegian Colony: Nick Olsen, Lawrence Pederson, Richard Pederson and Oscar Olsen. Along with the pole extension charge, the Oxnard Home Telephone Company charged a connection fee of $3.50 per house. Into the late 1940s, Uncle Neil recalls, the phone sat silently for days on end because everyone was afraid to use it. Grandpa and Nana had little reason to change their habits and didn't know too many people who had a phone.

During the war years, Grandpa manned the Civil Air Patrol telephone a few miles away in Santa Rosa Valley. He took turns with his neighbors on around-the-clock shifts. The government phone was not to be used for personal reasons. Volunteers served four-hour stints in the 5'x 8' shack at the Geery farm. Their job was to identify and report all aircraft that flew within their spotting area. Echo-Echo-Black was the code for that portion of the Conejo. For each shift, two spotters worked together. One called out the numbers painted on the bottom of a wing while the other manned the phone. Sometimes Grandpa and my mother shared shifts when she was in high school.

For post-WWII civil defense, Grandpa was required to keep in practice by recording all flights for a randomly selected twenty-four hour period. He kept his field glasses and an official flight manual near his back door. Whenever a plane flew overhead we were instructed to maintain strict silence so that he could concentrate. He took his duty seriously. His grandchildren thought that, during the war, he had single-handedly saved California from Japanese air attack.

Every farm needed a horse; at least Nana's father, Silas Kelley, thought so. For a few years he held a side job buying up old horses to feed to the lions at Louie Goble's burgeoning enterprise, the Lion Farm, in the yet-undeveloped area of Thousand Oaks. Nana didn't want a horse for her young daughters because she felt horses were dangerous and unpredictable. One day, Silas drove in with a pony in the back of his old truck. He felt like it had a few good years left in it, and his granddaughters needed it more than the lions did. Nana relented.

As teenagers, my mother and her sisters acquired Loretta, their mare, from the same source. By then the Lion Farm had become more sophisticated, with trained animal shows open to the public. Prior to being pink-slipped, Loretta was a rising star, a circus horse *par excellance*. Her job was to enter the circus ring pulling a cartload of barking seals while the crowds erupted in applause. But Loretta lacked a true performer's grit and harbored a fatal flaw. The horse was deathly afraid of elephants. Each time one trumpeted during a performance, Loretta bolted, toppling the seals. Louie Goble finally got tired of the pandemonium and sold her to Grandpa for fifty dollars.

My aunt Arthelia detested riding, so Loretta became my mother's horse. She rode it until she married. Then her younger sister assumed ownership.

A few years later, Grandpa acquired Ben, a tall, raw-boned gelding, in a similar manner. Grandpa was not fond of horses. He didn't ride for pleasure, but he trailered the horse around the southeastern part of the county while he poisoned ground squirrels for the Agricultural Department of Ventura County. Nana and Grandpa didn't possess fine bloodstock, but I learned that it is good to have a horse around.

A tack room stood in the farmyard, air-tight and infused with the odor of oats and mice. A hasp and lock fastened its door securely to protect the contents from theft. Bridles hung on neat pegs and saddles straddled saddle trees. Rows of curry combs and liniment bottles gave the tack room an ambiance that boosted Grandpa's standing beyond that of a mere sheep farmer. His tack room smelled of leather and horse sweat. Inside that room, we could imagine that Grandpa was like Nana's brothers, men of the West.

A few paces away Nana made her own soap in a dirt-floored wash room and ran her clothes through a 1938 Maytag washing machine. The room smelled like lye and Borax. Nana kept a small scissors nearby to snip oversized buttons off of garments before running them through the wringer and taking the chance of breaking them in half. I helped run the clothes through the wringer on the day she used her last bar of homemade soap and decided to switch to store-bought.

The wash room had a social beginning. As newlyweds, Nana and her sister-in-law, Babe, shared their best times while "making do". One of them owned an old wringer washing machine, the other, a two-cylinder gasoline motor that sputtered and belched fumes. Grandpa hooked the two together and built a washroom. Every Monday, Babe would bring her washing. She and Nana heated water, ran their laundry through the machine and retired to the house to eat lunch and visit until the clothes dried on the clothesline. The trousers and work clothes dried on branches of a pepper tree that grew conveniently gnarled and twisted because my aunt and my mother climbed it before it was strong enough to support them.

In my mind, the farm seemed inseparably defined by its trees. A stand of blue gum eucalyptus stood at the bottom of the hill, planted for firewood. The trees crowded together in splendid disarray. We children loved and feared them, these fearsome trees that poisoned the soil beneath so that even weeds could not grow. Heedless of the mess they strewed on the ground, their canopies blocked out the sun and reached as tall as the sky. When the wind blew, they writhed and moaned as their spindly trunks rubbed against each other, sixty feet up. The gum trees littered the ground with sweet-smelling leaves and hard seedpods that we collected for necklaces. The gumtree grove was the closest thing to a forest that we children had seen. The trees defied the rules of agrarian order, planted close together in hodgepodge fashion, not in neat, symmetrical rows like the apricot orchard that stood on another part of the farm.

Like my mother when she was my age, I recall standing at the perimeter of this random wood, trying to summon nerve to walk through the "forest". In our imaginations, a wolf or a tramp could be hiding within the dark shadows. It took more courage than I possessed to creep through its swaying maze. Only once did I take up my brother's dare to run through to the other side. Years later, I recalled the shrieking stand of eucalyptus when I watched a war movie, feeling a kinship with the soldiers in a distant rainforest.

If the blue gums provided fuel, the apricot and citrus orchards were the "cash cows" of the pre-war years. High school students vied for jobs pitting Grandpa's apricots every summer. The annual pitting provided an excuse for young people to camp out, build bonfires and talk into the night, meet prospective dates and earn spending money for school clothes. It was the equivalent of summer camp and homecoming week, a huge social rendezvous that cousins, into their old age, recalled as their favorite experience of the Conejo. Girls pitted (cut the apricots in half and lay the two pieces cup-side up on wooden trays to be moved into smudging sheds and sulfured as a means of preserving them). Boys picked fruit, carried the trays and spread the sulfured apricots to dry in the sun. After two days in the sun, the boys shoveled the dried fruit into burlap gunny sacks. It was eventually sold to dried fruit brokers and shipped out in boxcars from the Moorpark rail station.

In the era before refrigeration and electricity, dried apricots were a staple. They were candy, fruit and medicine all in one, a recommended cure for irregularity from a hard scrabble diet of beans and bread, a preventative of scurvy, and

15

a source of vitamins A and C among grain harvesting crews, and a sweet to be carried in the pocket for between meals.

Grandpa maintained an apiary of honeybees to pollinate his tree crops.

The farm was steeped in permanence. My great-grandfather, Nils, had owned the land even before my grandfather was born. We grandchildren enjoyed a luxury that might seem foreign in today's mobile society, the joy of sharing our mothers' toys and playhouse, her climbing tree and hayloft. We picked oranges and apricots from the same trees she did when she was our age. We rode her girlhood horse and slept in her old bed and shared her mother's attention. The bond of those events remains, even though Nana is gone. When my mother speaks of her childhood I am transported in place. I know of what she speaks. It serves as a reminder that life did not change greatly from her childhood to mine.

Nana's house seemed larger than its blueprints would indicate, but perhaps no house is big enough to store the wealth of memories that cluster within its walls. Although it is gone now, torn down in the name of progress, Nana's house was no exception.

Chapter Three
Lessons of Love

After her funeral, I found Nana's photograph album on a table, and I opened it to pages of black and white photographs. They contained snapshots of a time that I hadn't known existed. Her brothers in their younger years were a surprise; handsome, fun loving, with a look of ease that came from growing up without boundaries or restrictions.

Her sisters stood before the camera, slim, pretty, dressed in lovely serge and

Left to right; Fred Kelley, Walter Kelley, John Kelley, two friends, and Charlie Kelley.

crepe, with coils of chestnut hair. From under the brim of a white hat, Nana smiled with an expression that I recognize in myself.

I found another side of her in the photographs that lined the book; Nana in riding gear. I discovered that she had been an excellent horsewoman. Her daughters recall her riding even in her thirties—another misconception on my part. Grandpa had been the one who mistrusted horses. I knew Nana only as a grandmother, dressed in floral housedresses. It was hard to think of her in boots and split skirt, an early-day Dale Evans.

A snapshot of her in a photo booth at Pacific Ocean Park with her brothers recalled for me the day that my brother and I visited the same amusement park, forty years later.

The backgrounds of the photos showed places and houses that I recognized, but they seemed newly built, with sparse yards and porches and walls in need of paint. The flowers and refinements came later, when electricity and pumps and water hoses made landscaping practical.

Wedding photographs taken in backyards often included a chicken or two within the photo's frame (the free range chickens seemed to explain the sparse yards), or a row of tents pitched for guests to sleep in. I found an invitation to a wedding reception that instructed the bearer, presumably Nana, to bring silverware and cups for the dinner.

Nana and Grandpas' wedding photo, taken on the Kelley Ranch with her brother John and cousin Irene. Left to right: John, Irene, Nana, Oscar

I was not alone in searching the photographs for subtle overtones of a bygone age. An elderly cousin recounted her memories of Nana as we turned the pages of an album, and I was grateful for the gift that she gave me; her memories of my Nana at sixteen. She had attended Timber School with both Nana and Grandpa. As she told it, Grandpa stopped the other boys, including Nana's brothers, from pulling Nana's pigtails. The elderly cousin filled the gaps, answered questions that I had forgotten to ask Nana. Years later, she explained, my grandparents met again at the Ventura County Fair. Nana's father gave permission for Grandpa to drive her home. Later, when her father, Silas, gave his permission, he came courting.

Nana's brothers liked Oscar. He was a plain faced, serious Norwegian with a two-hundred acre farm. He owned a 1910 Samson tractor, one of the first in the Conejo, and sixty head of cattle. More surprisingly, Nana's father liked Oscar more than her other callers.

Nana had shared stories that the photographs gave no hint of. She had been courted by a wagoneer, a feisty German ten years her senior named Frank Fritchle, until her father ran him off in order to give Grandpa a clear field. Years later, Fritchle's niece married Nana's son, my Uncle Neil. We called Mr. Fritchle "Uncle", and my mother cared for him in his later years until his death.

Nana's new boyfriend bore the brunt of her brothers' Irish pranks. Four brothers and a host of cousins seemed an uneven match against one Norwegian. Quiet and shy, unused to children or sisters, Grandpa made an easy target for practical jokes.

Once he came calling in a horse and buggy, and Nana's brothers hoisted the buggy onto the barn. Another time, when he drove the Overland automobile that he shared with his brother, Nana's brothers rolled it into a dry creek bed. He had to return to the house and ask Silas to hitch a mule to the front bumper to pull it from the gully. It was nearly midnight before he set off for home.

When he brought candy, Nana's little sisters rushed to grab the sack before he could knock on the door. For three straight Saturdays the same thing happened. He solved his dilemma by showing up on the fourth week with two bags of candy, one for the little girls, another for Nana.

The pranks weren't limited to Nana's brothers. The first two times Grandpa came calling, he spent the evening in the living room, visiting with Nana's father and brothers while she finished the dishes. As soon as she dried her hands and hung the towel to dry, her father consulted his watch and announced, "Time for bed." After that, Grandpa learned to help her do the dishes; at least they could visit while they worked.

After a year of courting, Grandpa stopped coming. For three months he stayed away—all summer. Nana's family thought they had gone too far with their practical jokes and Nana's mother made her husband ride over to the Norwegian Colony to find out whether Grandpa had lost interest. Silas returned home with Grandpa's promise that he would resume his courtship after the grain and beans were harvested.

The photographs in the albums provided a record of my grandparent's courtship, a love connection in the turning pages that grew with the passing years. Looking on, I knew the feeling of children watching their parents waltzing around the kitchen in the dark, kissing when they thought no one was looking. By the time I was aware of them as a couple, Nana and Grandpa were in their late fifties and had a pragmatic, comfortable marriage with the rough edges long since worn away. I had no way of judging the depth of their affection for each other. Beyond Grandpa's occasional pat on Nana's shoulder, they were not given to public displays.

The pictorial record included a happy ending, a photo that stunned me with its honesty. It was of Nana at twenty-one, clad in her wedding dress, sitting back on a wooden trunk, laughing in absolute delight. She shone like a pixie, pretty, happy, happy. I had always wondered if Nana, the most serious of her brothers and sisters, had chosen Grandpa because he was the only one who offered. They seemed so serious and task-driven that I feared they might have settled for convenience. But in the photo, her face radiated with anticipation and joy.

Proof again of their commitment shows in a photograph of them standing on a porch, Nana leaning into Grandpa's shoulder, young, in love, expecting the best from their lives together. In the photos, I found the answer to a lifetime question. Love was a family heritage.

In another photograph, Grandpa, staunch and rock solid in his lifetime, stood alongside his motorcycle. Hurrah, we came from adventurous stock.

Oscar Olsen with his Indian Motorcycle, 1918.

Honeymoons end. The album showed the story, or maybe it posed questions that needed answers from those who were there. Maybe courtship is like eating dessert first. The substance comes later. For Nana and Grandpa, duties and distance prevented them from getting to know each other well before their marriage. It took a while for them—two stubborn individualists—to get used to each other's ways. For a year or two they must have rubbed like two stiff shoes.

A single frame showed a stern woman standing beside my six-year-old mother and my nine-year-old aunt. Unhappiness filled her eyes. Despair convoluted her features. I asked my mother who she was, this woman with my great-grandmother's eyes.

One afternoon my mother provided the answer. It was Nana. There had been another son, born in 1930 when my mother was five, a firstborn son who carried Grandpa's name, Ivan Oscar. In old-world tradition, he was to be the heir to Grandpa's land and fortunes.

As a young Lutheran courting an Irish Catholic girl, Grandpa confronted the inflexible power of the Holy Roman Church. He converted to Catholicism and signed a paper stating that the children of the union would be raised Catholic. I can only guess that the condition galled him like a sore as he endured the murmurings of his Lutheran relatives. He remained steadfast in his promise through the birth of two daughters, but he decided that his son would be baptized Lutheran in his family's tradition. Nana found herself in the position of Catholic women throughout the ages, fearful that only Catholic babies go to Heaven.

With ironic tragedy, the baby died a few hours after birth. He was baptized by a nun in St. John's Hospital and buried in a plain grave in the Santa Clara cemetery, in a heartrending service that gave neither peace nor resolution to the grieving parents. My mother remembers her mother crying inconsolably, her father awkwardly patting her mother's shoulder, unable to vent the despair that lined his face. She said it was the saddest funeral she ever attended.

A few months later, Grandpa formed a cement headstone in his workshop and they returned to the cemetery to set it in place. But the ground had been disked over, the metal marker that designated the baby's grave, lost. They could not find the spot.

Years later, the baby's sister, my aunt Mary Rydberg, persisted in her efforts to find the location. She was told that the old Monsignor who had been in charge of burials kept few records, mostly in his head. He was long dead and could be of no use in the search. Finally, when it became obvious that Aunt Mary wouldn't give up, the cemetery clerk admitted that, in the infant section of the Montalvo Cemetery, the babies' graves had been covered over and another layer buried on top. There was no way to know where the baby lay buried.

Baby Oscar's marker was never set in place. It remained in his father's workshop until Oscar, Sr. died. Today, it graces his sister's reflection garden.

Mental depression had not made its way into household jargon; a baby's death was something that a woman was expected to overcome. I don't know if

Grandpa ever understood the guilt that Nana bore over losing her baby twice, once to death and a second time in the quiet graveyard. It is not difficult to imagine her thoughts as she searched the rows of unmarked graves where her baby lay,

Nana (Theresa Kelley Olsen) on her wedding day, 1921.

lost to her forever. She had failed to deliver him to Heaven's gates.

Two more babies, Mary and Neil, were born many years later, presumably when forgiveness was asked for and received. Both were baptized in the Catholic Church.

As the wounds from the loss of her baby healed, the Church continued to exert its influence on Nana. She accepted Mass as an obligation, but barely tolerated the handshaking and relaxed attitudes that came in the '70s. It seemed to me that she kept her religion at a distance. She invited the priests to occasional barbecues and wedding feasts without relying on them to provide solutions to problems that she could settle herself.

Whatever her feelings about the past may have been, Nana lived and died a good Catholic. In the hospital room, the day that her grandsons and I gathered around with our mothers, it was the rosary that brought us together. We prayed over and over, "Hail Mary, Mother of God...pray for us sinners now and at the hour of our death. Hail Mary...pray for us sinners now and at the hour of our death." Beneath Nana's closed eyes, a tear slipped down her cheek and disappeared in the fold of her neck.

Some years earlier, in 1983, when my father passed away without warning, Nana's heart nearly broke with sadness for my mother. She sobbed over and over, "Why wasn't it me? I've been ready to go since Oscar died. Why wasn't it me?"

In his seventies, Grandpa turned to the Church and became close friends with his parish priest. During the last year of his life the two men passed many rainy afternoons in conversation about farming, travel, and the nature of life. Grandpa died in 1972. Nana outlived him by fifteen lonely years.

Nana's world opened to me at the time when I would have attended kindergarten had such an opportunity been available. But Conejo School did not introduce its first kindergarten until the following year. A child enters its fifth year with a curiosity and a hunger for the world beyond nursery doors.

When I was born, my grandmother was delighted. I was named for her. Nana was curious, hardworking and sensible, attributes mirrored in me, her first granddaughter. After I was old enough to be good company, I began to visit Nana and we began a lifelong friendship.

In the pre-television world of the early 1950s, children's social knowledge seemed largely limited to the physical world around them. That world still included cousins and grandparents. Nana's ways were different from my mother's and I studied those differences intently, choosing, judging, and weighing each advantage. My mother grew up seeking approval from her own mother that she felt eluded her. I had no such complaint.

Nana drove a De Soto, a dark blue sedan with leather seats and a tight chassis. Its motor purred above the sound of tires on the gravel driveway. If the car had a radio, it was not used. The automobile was used for important occasions:

the weekly trip to town or the occasional visit to relatives—never for spur-of-the-moment runs to the market for ice cream. The De Soto was housed in a detached shed behind the gum tree grove, a tiny garage of corrugated tin that squeezed the De Soto's sides so tightly we could scarcely slide into the car.

Before plucking the ignition key from her handbag she donned white gloves and tucked her skirts beneath her on the bench seat. Her passengers did not eat in her automobile. To my knowledge, no gum wrapper or paper scrap ever found its way into her car. Seventeen years later, when the car was retired with a cracked block, it was in nearly pristine condition.

Nana drove with the caution of someone who learned to drive as an adult. She grasped the steering wheel with both hands, drove at forty-five miles an hour, and allowed little conversation while she concentrated on the road. I was surprised to learn that, at fourteen, she drove all over Los Angeles, acting as her mother's chauffeur. In her youth, Nana had been issued a lifetime driver's license, the same as everyone was in those days. A few years later she lost her handbag and had to reapply for a new license. By then the State of California had changed its policy and no longer issued lifetime passes. Her new one stipulated that she had to reapply every few years like the rest of us.

Chapter Four
Land of Our Fathers' Pride

German Pragmatists

Los Angeles sprawl eventually devoured the Conejo Valley, but in its glory days thousands of acres lay in flat bottomland, surrounded by whale-humped knolls covered with native grasses that had never felt the cut of till or furrow.

During 1860, William H. Brewer, on his first geological survey through California, passed through a lovely valley on his way from the San Fernando Valley to Buenaventura. It was bordered on all sides by rugged mountains and exited by a steep grade that tested the skills of his wagoneer, Jack. Brewer's path took him through the Rancho Trifuno. Within a few days he had passed through the valley on his way to other vistas and his journey through the "beautiful valley" was distilled to little more than a paragraph in his journal.

The Valley had been home to the Chumash Indians who gathered acorns from a thousand oaks and left their mark gently on the land. As a former land grant, it had been deeded to the great José de la Guerra by the Spanish government when a former owner abandoned interest in the valley. Caspar Borchard, Sr. settled in the Conejo after traveling there by a circuitous route, beckoned from Germany by the promise of good land.

It was bottomland that Caspar Borchard, Sr. purchased from the bank in the mid 1800s, land repossessed from James Hammell in a drought year, shortly after he also lost his Grand Union Hotel in Newbury Park. The land must have been a bargain for a farmer with a number of lively sons to help out.

The family used the surrounding hillsides to raise goats (at one time 1,700) and sheep. They built out-buildings for a slaughtering and meat-cutting business. They planted fields to pasture for their herd of a hundred horses, which includ-

25

ed huge draft horses from stock that Caspar brought from Germany. Farmers came from far distances to purchase them for pulling their threshing machines.

The flatland yielded its promise in wet years and in dry. An experimental farmer, Borchard introduced crops that were new to the area: tomatoes, giant pumpkins, walnuts, grain. He made charcoal from the smaller oaks and planted apricot trees on some of the cleared land.

In late summer, the Borchards operated a threshing machine. A huge rig probably owned by a neighbor named Wadde, it was pulled by twenty-six horses in four rows, six abreast. Two of the most trusted served as lead team. They moved it around to thresh barley and wheat on neighbors' farms. The older boys traded responsibility for handling the reins, a muscle-wrenching activity that taxed their physical strength and required a deep understanding of equine psychology.

Each fall brought the end of the growing season. When the residents of the Conejo came together to dance and make merry, it was most often in Caspar, Sr.'s barn, just before the new hay or grain crop was laid up on the smooth floors. Local musicians took turns playing their instruments while farmers and their wives danced and took potluck dinner, and their babies slept on blankets in the corner.

The early history of the Conejo was marked with stories of boom and bust. The Grand Hotel failed when the stagecoach route was diverted to the Santa Rosa Valley. Later, the railroad bypassed the area in favor of the Simi Valley, where a line connected Ventura to the Los Angeles basin without the barrier of mountains. Drought and disease bested the efforts of struggling farmers and stockmen. Farms changed hands as owners sold out, went broke or moved on. The inhabitants of the Conejo seemed to change with the whims of fortune. The spoils did not necessarily go to those who arrived first, but to those who held on the longest.

Through this period, Caspar, Sr.'s methodical practices allowed him to add to the family holdings. At one time he owned ten thousand acres in Ventura County, perhaps a like amount in Orange County, and two ranches in Texas that totaled eight thousand acres.

In 1918 he retired. His wealth was sufficient that he gifted each of his eight children with $12,000 and 2000 acres. Taking them to the top of the Conejo Grade, he pointed out how he planned to divide the land using creeks, roads and natural boundaries.

Four of the boys, Frank, Antone, Charles and Leo chose to make their homes on the family land around Santa Ana, in Orange County. Rosa, Teresa, Mary and

Caspar, Jr. remained in the Conejo. By the time I came into the family, these four (excluding Mary, who never married) had retired, and their sons were farming and ranching the land.

The four brothers who moved to Santa Ana sometimes returned with their families for weekend visits. So numerous had the family grown that even a casual visit became a family reunion whenever two or more generations chanced to bring potluck and stop by for a day of visiting.

In later years, some of the orange groves the Borchards planted in Santa Ana were condemned under the laws of public domain. When construction began at the onset of World War II, the land was needed to build an Air Force base and later, to construct the Santa Ana Freeway. I remember the family's astonishment when Antone was compensated for the loss of his orange trees at the rate of $1,500 per tree, the value calculated over its projected lifetime. The orchard rows were long and contained many trees; the State of California did well by the Santa Ana Borchards.

The children of Caspar Borchard, Sr. were content with their holdings. According to his daughter Teresa, none felt that one had benefited to the detriment of the others. They were happy with each other's successes, prone to offer advice and to learn from each other. They raised their children with a respect for the numerous aunts and uncles, and strong familial ties endured into the present generations.

Gentleness was a birthright that we acquired, one generation bequeathing it to another. The family heeded lessons taught by Caspar, Sr. Farming, by its very nature, had enough competition from the insects and the weather. It did not need squabbling among its members. Chance favored the hardest working; there was opportunity enough for all and cooperation increased the chances for success.

When development finally

*Five generations of Borchards;
From left, rear row, John Kelley, Nana front
row Rosa Kelley, Caspar Borchard, Sr.
Holding Granddaughters Catherine and
Arthelia*

came, the remaining farmers sold their land for more than their grandest dreams. Often this meant that some farmers benefited more than others—those who were willing to work harder, or those blessed with better luck, or those families with strong sons and daughters that worked the farms without compensation until better times arrived. It was so with my family.

Teresa married a distant cousin from the wealthy "Cincinnati Borchards". Her new husband, Edward, had attended business college, and he attacked the challenge of farming with practicality and innovation. He was an excellent judge of stock, raised cattle and horses on several thousand acres of owned and leased land while planting over twelve hundred acres to walnuts and grain. During his stewardship, he farmed his sister-in-law Mary's land as well.

In 1940 he retired, and his sons Robert and Edward, Jr. formed a partnership, the Borchard Brothers Ranch. Their younger brother, Allen, joined them when he returned from World War II. Quiet, serious men, they spent most of their time on their tractors and in their fields. For those of us who lived closer to town, their presence was evident each summer when the corner of Newbury Park and Borchard Roads abounded with their lush red tomatoes destined for the Hunts Packing Company.

The Borchard brothers employed an old man as a watchman of sorts, letting him live in an old sheepherder's wagon at the back of their walnut orchard. Perhaps a hired hand that had grown too old to work, he lived as a hermit. I joined my cousins in thinking he was some sort of boogieman. Known only as Harvey, he became a sort of folk legend, a solitary man who talked to himself and shunned his neighbors. Reed-thin, hunched and unwashed, with dirty clothes that reeked, he had a scraggly, gray beard and sharp, piercing eyes. We hid behind fences and haystacks and watched in clandestine silence as he passed down the road.

Every Wednesday morning at 10:00 a.m., Harvey passed our house on his five-mile trek into Newbury Park for groceries. Unless he caught a ride with one of the Borchard men, we saw him walking home in the late afternoon, his gunnysack filled with provisions. Summer or winter, his routine never varied.

One day in early spring, he failed to return home. The nights were cold, and we knew he was in trouble. The sheriff mounted a search and rescue. The Borchard brothers interrupted their farming to comb the area in pickups and on horseback. Neighbor joined neighbor to search for a man that many us had considered a nuisance.

He was found weeks later in the hills behind the Hunt Ranch, dead from exposure. He had apparently become disoriented and wandered off looking for his home. For a long time afterwards I watched for him on Wednesday mornings. Something fundamental seemed to disappear with his passing.

The residents of Borchard Road kept an eye out for strangers. It was a long, sparsely populated road, and we knew everyone who belonged. Strangers afoot (with the exception of Harvey) were escapees from Camarillo State Hospital. Everyone called them "nuts". The first person to spot a walk-away made a phone call to the hospital and another to her nearest neighbor. The phone chain followed the stranger all the way to the highway, warning mothers to gather their children and lock their doors.

The Borchard Brothers Ranch flourished until Teresa and her three sons sold it in 1962. Teresa moved from the ranch house (where she had lived since her marriage in 1912) to a house on Oak Street in Camarillo across from her daughter. She worried at first about the transition, but found that town living appealed to her. Ironically, she lived out her last years on the site of her old Home Place, at Mary Health of the Sick Convalescent Hospital on Borchard Road.

Her sons moved away as well, two of them to farms in Winters and one to Salinas, and continued to farm tomatoes and row crops. They continued their Grandfather Caspar, Sr.'s tradition of raising huge pumpkins. Some years we saw their photographs in UPI newspaper articles when they won the world's largest pumpkin growing contest.

Two years after the Borchards settled in the Conejo, a widower named John Reily Kelley brought his motherless children from Nebraska and purchased four hundred acres of farmland from Caspar, Sr. Local history seems to credit Caspar, Sr. with settling the Conejo, (and rightfully so with his huge land acquisitions), but John Reily was a valued and respected member of the community. His big black stallion, his scientific farming methods and his affable offspring were widely known.

John Reily Kelley's family settled in 1889 and put down long roots. His son Silas married one of Caspar's daughters, Rosa—my great-grandmother—and began raising cattle and hogs.

Norwegian Colonists

In 1886, five young men made the trip from Norway by way of Ellis Island and the Union Pacific Railroad. Friends and relatives from Stranda, an area along the Störfjord, they came without wives. Most left fiancées waiting in Norway for them to find a safe location. Karen (Norwegian spelling, Karn), Lars Pederson's intended, had heard stories of the wild and woolly West and instructed him to go ahead and check things out. If it seemed safe, he could return for her and she would marry him. True to his word he eventually did. But for four years the bachelor men settled in Santa Barbara. They met a labor broker and banker who helped them find skilled work and they saved everything they earned. Their reputation as workers served them well. Industrious from birth, Norwegians gained a reputation for taking pride in their work and being eager learners.

My Great-grandfather, Nils Olsen, (pronounced Niles; born Nils Uren until the immigration people renamed him "Olsen") hailed from Ura, Norway. He worked as a stonemason on the renovation of the Santa Barbara Mission, where he rebuilt the mission walls. Later, he created the stonework along State Street.

In 1888, the Norwegians heard that George Edwards, a son of one of the original settlers, had land for sale from the former Rancho El Conejo. They purchased Section 28 as a whole, each man putting his money into the kitty.

The land was divided into parcels which lay side by side, some better than others. When it came time to assign ownership of the parcels, all put their names into a hat. The rules were simple: each man would draw lots. The legal plots would be allocated in numerical order per the land map. They decided against each man making a random choice. They wanted no hard feelings between them; the outcome would be determined by luck of the draw.

Ole Anderson drew first, for lot number one, 199 acres containing the Indian Cliffs. Lars Pederson drew next for 111 acres of prime bottomland. Ole Nilson drew for 97 acres. George Hansen drew for the 105-acre lot, and finally, Nils Olsen earned the remaining 139 acres by process of elimination.

The men had worked hard to make the division equitable. There was some grumbling by those who ended up with the rocky perimeters while others won the fertile "flats", but the land was divided so that each got a portion of the prime tilling land. Maybe because he was upset with the rockiness of his plot, Ole Anderson remained in Santa Barbara and never farmed his acreage.

Lars Pederson returned to Norway to collect the fiancées. The four women decided that it would be safer to travel under his protection, so they hurried their affairs and returned to California on the same ship. Within a few months, everyone but Ole Anderson had married.

The land must have seemed like paradise to families used to ten months of snow. Nils was moved to remark, upon first seeing his new home, "There sure is a lot of rocks and sage brush here!"

Regardless of each family's holdings, they worked equally long hours. Soon after sunrise each could look across his land and see his neighbors plowing or reaping. Hard labor made for democracy in the fields. The Norwegians remained friends and relied on each other for everything from camaraderie in their mother tongue to spare parts for harness and plow.

In December of 1900, the first rains of the season came with frightening force, bringing a cyclone at 3:00 o'clock in the morning while Lina and George (Jorgen) Hansen were asleep in their one-room shanty. They awakened to find their roof blown off and raindrops falling on their heads. Wind tore the side-walls, and they collapsed outward, leaving the Hansens awake and soaked in their double bed, in the middle of a violent storm. As she later recorded in her diary, Mrs. Hansen groped in the darkness for her shoes and threw a dirty rug over her sodden nightshirt. She and her husband walked through the storm toward a light they saw flickering in the Pederson's window.

Lars Pederson set off by horseback to collect his neighbors. Within half an hour, Ole Nelson and Nils Olsen brought lanterns and returned with Jorgen to the house. In darkness and rain, they collected food, clothing, and bedding, and stored it in the barn under cover from the storm. Most of the dishes had been smashed, but an unbroken crock contained cracked chicken and duck eggs. Daylight saw the neighbors sharing a breakfast of scrambled eggs before they separated for their own homes and chores.

Within days the house was rebuilt reusing the original walls, in a more protected spot near a grove of willow trees. The roof was found lying nearby and was reattached. Mrs. Hansen had a time scrubbing the men's muddy footprints off the walls and ceiling. But she praised God that the chickens and cows were safe. God had spared their lives and made everything good again. They were well satisfied.

The Mediterranean climate and rainfall of the Conejo became sources of both satisfaction and puzzlement to the Norwegians. They wrote letters home to Norway about the abundant land and the ease of farming. On years when the rains fell, they drove wagonloads of hay and beans to Oxnard and Hueneme by way of the Potrero Grade, a steep grade that links modern day Newbury Park to the plains south of Camarillo. On the two-day, trip, the farmers left the Norwegian Colony at daybreak and arrived in Hueneme in the late afternoon. They unloaded, stayed overnight, and departed for home the following morning. The beans were destined to be loaded onto sailing ships, the hay sold to liveries and horse ranches on the Oxnard plain. To make it over the steep grade, the men set their brakes or lashed a tree limb through the rear wheels while a team of horses dragged the load to the bottom of the hill.

In those years when the rains didn't come, the Norwegians fretted, mended harness and scratched the adobe soil to break the surface for their withering seedlings, and waited for the next season. The journals of the early farmers recorded careful notations of the rainfall. They tried to discern the weather patterns of their strange new land where winter did not bring snow.

For thirteen years, the original five farmers worked their soil, but their way was not without tragedy. George Hansen was gravely injured, his spine broken when a young wagon handler, probably one of the hired men, forgot to set the wagon brake near the Potrero Grade and the horses and wagons went over the side. George was so badly injured that he spent a year in bed. History doesn't record how a man curses his stupidity while the seasons cycle and his lands are farmed by neighbors. They had burdens enough of their own without adding his.

In 1909, another Norwegian youth was handling a rig. Two wagons were being pulled by a team of six horses down the same grade. A 28-year-old hired man, Martin Peterson, rode behind, handling the long-handled wooden brake on the second wagon. At the bottom of the grade, at a dry wash called the Arroyo Simi, they had to cross a steep bank, ford the creek bed and climb the other side. Something caught the brake lever that Martin was holding and caused him to flip onto the ground. He fell in front of a wagon wheel, unnoticed, and the wagon rolled over him.

Immediately afterwards the driver saw that Martin was seriously hurt. Gingerly, he picked him up and placed him in the wagon. He stopped for help at the first house they came to, the Daily residence in Camarillo where they normally watered their horses. The injured man was carried inside and attended to while the young farmer rushed to Camarillo to unload the wagons. When he returned, Peterson was dead.

Martin Peterson was buried in the Olsen Family Cemetery. Oscar Olsen lost his best friend. The young man driving the wagon was Grandpa.

From 1893 to 1912, illnesses struck one family with no explanation. Nils and Ellen Olsen lost seven of their ten children to a baffling illness that weakened their muscles and left them bedridden. Except for one son who died of the disease, it was the daughters who perished. Each in turn showed signs of illness and began a slow decline. Sometimes the girls took two years to become bedridden and die. Most were born healthy and lived to ages of between five and ten. A few were born sickly and had difficulty learning to walk; these died younger. Others lived healthily for five or eight years before developing symptoms. Each time one of her children began to stiffen and sicken, Mother Ellen tried every home remedy that she or her neighbors could think to apply. Doctors came from Oxnard on several occasions.

No one ever discovered the source of the illness; some claimed that it was tuberculosis. Some felt that it was rheumatic fever, others blamed the fact that Ellen fed her children Eagle Brand and the children didn't get enough vitamins. Some felt that anemia was the culprit.

A web of shame and guilt wrapped the family at something they could not control. The non-English speaking Norwegians already seemed clannish and odd to their American neighbors. All over the valley people gossiped about the probable causes of the children's deaths. Aunt Jenny, Ellen's relative, held one opinion: possibly Nil's land was to blame. Nils's relatives, the Hansens, held another view that criticized the children's mother.

Karen Pederson was the midwife who attended the children's births. As an old woman she recalled to her daughter-in-law, Vida, that she could tell when they were born, which children would later die because they were born with a stiff spine. Some couldn't walk or took a long time to learn. All became crippled and bedridden in the last year of their life. The last child's cause of death was listed as tuberculosis. In later years, medical doctors have suggested that the others died of tuberculin meningitis.

It is ironic that Thora, the last victim, might not have died from meningitis at all, but from tuberculosis contracted from a hired man who lived with them.

In their diaries, the Norwegian women mentioned their feeling that God's will dictated their lives and deaths. Their deeply-held faith allowed them to harbor no bitterness towards those who might inadvertently bring them disease.

Seven times, Nils Olsen made a small wooden casket, which Ellen lined with flannel, and together with her said prayers over a grave. When the weather allowed, someone rode to Moorpark for a preacher. Nils Olsen buried his seven children in a homemade cemetery at the end of the road that later bore his name. For years, until the sun and rain deteriorated them, the markers were lined in neat rows: Paula, age ten, died 1893; Nora, age six, died 1900; Emma, age seven, died 1903; Nora, age five, died 1905; Laura, age seven, died 1908; Ned, age eight, died 1911; Thora, age seven, died 1912.

Only Oscar Ivan, born between Nora and Emma, Peder Ludvik (Ludwick,) born between Emma and the second Nora, and Nicolay (Nicholas, or Nick), born last, survived.

My mother often rode her horse to the end of the lane in the late afternoons and climbed the little fence to sit at the graves of her aunts and uncle.

My grandfather spoke little of those events to his own children, even more rarely to his grandchildren. Those of us who learned of it sensed his pain and knew to leave his private sorrow alone. Years later, he recalled his mother rocking the sick children, singing a Norwegian lullaby, "Last year, I herded the sheep on the hills. This year, I rock my baby in the cradle."

Grandpa kept a small card hidden in his dresser, on which he had glued the cut-out figures of two little girls from a mail order catalogue, life-like dolls with long blonde curls and bonnets, and a small donkey. As an adult he moved it to his desk where it stayed until he died. It was his grief card, the only image he had to remind him of his sisters.

Ellen Olsen died in August 1923, in her early fifties. In a quiet conversation she told Nana that she was ready to die, that her daughters were all dead and she had nothing to live for. The coroner's report cited heart disease. Perhaps her heart was merely broken. She was buried in Ivy Lawn Memorial Park in Ventura.

In 1901, Ole Anderson, George Hansen and Lars Pederson succumbed during a typhoid epidemic. The men were working near Filmore when they drank water from a well in which, after their deaths, a dead squirrel was found. The three men died within the week. Two of George Hansen's children succumbed as well, Grandpa's playmates. Again, speculation played its part in ascribing cause to the deaths. Some of the neighbors maintained that the men's deaths were the result of bad water, metals or alkali. Local gossip suggested deliberate poisoning.

When Mrs. Hansen traveled to Moorpark to pick up her husband's casket from the train, she found her sister, Susie, on the same sad errand. Their husbands had died on the same day, from having drunk from the well. Mrs. Hansen and her remaining daughter returned to Norway. She continued to write to her former neighbors and missed the Conejo all the rest of her life. A photograph of the Hansen family hangs in the Stagecoach Inn Museum, a beautiful, hopeful family dressed in fine clothes.

The Norwegian Colony had been dealt a deathblow.

After the Hansen's death, Nils Olsen bought their land in 1904 for $3,300 and Anderson's land for $1,500; a total of 304 acres for $4,800 which amounted to $15.79 per acre. This brought his holdings to 443 acres.

A few years later, the Ole Nilsen family moved to Northern California during an exceptionally dry year and the Pedersons purchased their land. By 1906, of the original five immigrant families, only two remained on the land.

After Lar's death, Karen Pederson, his widow, moved her three sons and daughter to Santa Barbara, to be nearer her beloved Lutheran Church and her friends. She bought a smaller farm and leased out her Conejo land until her sons were old enough to farm. Petite, blue-eyed and filled with a sense of humor, Karen earned a good living working as a housekeeper for a wealthy family in Santa Barbara. She had been employed in a similar manner before her marriage and became such a well-loved member of the household that her employers, the Salamos Family, hired a tutor to teach her English. She studied their cultured manners and raised her three sons and daughter in a refined manner that some-times caused misunderstandings among her neighbors on Olsen Road.

When her sons were scarcely teenagers, she sold her Santa Barbara farm and returned to the Conejo. She used the money from the sale of the Santa Barbara farm to drill a deep well and plant citrus in the Norwegian Colony.

A few years older than my grandfather, the Pederson brothers, Lawrence, Rich and Peder, became his life-long neighbors. Rich finally married when he was 65. Peder married Francis Larson and they had no children. Lawrence married at a younger age. He and his wife, Vida, had a daughter, Janet (Reeling). Vida and Nana became friends and Janet played with my Aunt Mary.

Only Rich served in the military, in World War I. He was proud of his serv-ice to his country and belonged to the American Legion for his entire life. Grandpa Olsen received his draft card, but missed serving when the war ended before his number was called.

In the Norwegian Colony, names were apparently less important to their bear-ers than to the outside world. The Norwegians knew their neighbors. If others had need to contact them, pretty close was close enough. Nil's father had been Ole. When Nils came to America, he became "Ole's son", or "Olsen". Ellen

Fjorstad was given the name 'Iverson' by the immigration officials and later married Nils Olsen. When Karen married Lars Berge (from the Norwegian district of Stranda), he had already changed his name to Pederson. Sometimes his name appears on official records as Lars Pederson Berge. Jorgen Overaa became George Hansen, although his neighbors continued to call him Jorgen.

Normally the vowel 'e' denotes persons of Norwegian birth, the letter 'o', Swedish, but this convention was not uniformly applied by the immigration officials. In official records, Ludwick Olsen's name appears at various times as Ludvic, Ludvick, Ludvig, Ludwick, Ludwig. His family called him Lud. Oscar Ivan Olsen's name appears on various documents as either Oscar Ivan or Ivan Oscar.

The Norwegians were as practical about their religion as they were about their names. When a preacher passed through the Conejo, they held service. When any of them traveled to Santa Barbara, they attended the Lutheran Church and noted in their diaries their pleasure at being able to do so. The rest of the time they attended the Methodist Church in Moorpark. Years later, Nil's funeral was held there.

Perhaps because I knew the story, I have always associated the lowly pepper tree with the sorrows of the Norwegian Colony. The Brazilian pepper trees that the early settlers planted must have seemed a strange substitute for the evergreens of Norway, but the trees flourished in drought years and in wet. The birds spread the seeds and today the narrow-leafed, crooked pepper trees can be found along fence lines throughout the Conejo.

Although there is some dispute among local historians about whether the Butterfield Stage actually ran through the Conejo, the Norwegians knew it to be so. It traveled on a narrow track that ran from the Stage Coach Inn, overland to the Norwegian Colony, cutting over the hill in a rocky crossing between Hansen's and Nilsen's properties. The narrow ledge was still visible until the 1950s, when bulldozers cleared the land to build houses.

One side of the hill had been built up with rocks so that the stagecoach did not list toward the downward slope. The wash at the base of the hill was likewise filled in with large rocks to provide a crossing. After passing over the hills, the trail zigzagged through the Tierra Rejada between the present site of the Santa Rosa School and the McCrea Ranch. After the dangerous passage, the trail leveled off to Simi. For Norwegians with only a smattering of English at the time, there was no reason for them to refer to the track as the Butterfield Stage Road unless it had been so.

Before 1911, wagons could travel no further than Olsen Road because a steep, rocky incline blocked access to the Santa Rosa Valley. The train stopped in Moorpark or Simi. The farmers of the valley were tired of hauling their hay down the steep switchbacks of the Conejo Grade or the out-of-the-way Potrero Grade on the west side of the valley. They wanted a shorter route to drive their cattle and haul their crops to Moorpark and the Simi Valley.

After Mr. Hansen was injured on the Potrero Grade, the Norwegians began work on a new grade, down the mountain that connected the Conejo to the Santa Rosa Valley. All the Norwegian men worked on it from time to time, and made a narrow track down the mountain.

In 1909, Nils Olsen, his sons and his hired men were the only ones still farming in the Norwegian Colony and they decided the road needed to be wider. They used a horse-drawn grader, picks and shovels, and sixty dollars worth of dynamite donated by Ventura County.

The road took two years to build, during breaks from their farming. It became their enduring contribution to Conejo Valley history. Their work cut the two-day trip to Hueneme, over the Potrero Grade to a day, with less danger to man and beast. Ellen Olsen thought to take a photograph of the auspicious event: the making of the Norwegian Grade. The photograph now hangs in the Stagecoach Inn Museum in Newbury Park. Ole Nielsen set the charges. My grandfather is the lad in the middle. His younger brother, Nicolas, was the water boy.

Only Lud, Oscar and Nicholas lived into adulthood. Lud farmed in partnership with Oscar for many years. Both of them courted at the same time. When it came time to wed, they divided their land in equal portions and continued to farm, side-by-side.

Later, Lud leased out his land to the others and moved to Santa Barbara when

Nana, her brother John, and Ethel Haigh, owner of the Stagecoach Inn.

his wife tired of rural life. He and Hazel later divorced. A small piece in the Star Free Press noted that Hazel was seeking a divorce on the grounds that Lud struck her with a 2"x4" scantling (piece of wood) and that he kicked her shins and neglected to bathe for periods extending over six months. They had lived together for nine years. The article noted that she asked for alimony.

Although my mother recalls another side to Lud's story that apparently involved Hazel, men, wine and song, Hazel obtained her divorce and presumably, Lud got his bath. He died in 1947 from stomach cancer and left no children. His stepson, Robert McAfee, Jr. eventually inherited his stepfather's land and converted the chicken pens that stood on his property into apartments that remain today.

When Nils Olsen died in 1940, he left his Moorpark property to his grandchildren. Three granddaughters inherited lots that he had purchased for ten dollars each or traded for a ton of hay. His two grandsons each inherited a house. Uncle Neil was four when he inherited a small house next door to the Catholic Church. His father rented it for him and deposited the three dollars monthly rent in a savings account that he was not allowed to touch. Later, the rent was raised to ten dollars. In the mid 1950s, when he was a senior in high school, Neil and Grandpa spent part of a summer putting in a bathroom to replace the outhouse. The rent was raised to thirty-five dollars.

The Olsens at home in the Norwegian Colony. Left, Nana holding Neil, Arthelia beside her grandfather Nils. Front, Mary, my mother Jean, cousin Nelda (in Nil's shadow), and Grandpa Oscar(holding hat).

Grandpa's younger brother, Nicolas (Nick) Olsen, tall, good looking and a natural athlete, intended to break the family farming tradition and get a "town job". He met his future wife, Sarah, at Moorpark High School. They made a pact; he would attend Santa Barbara State College (later UCSB) to become a high school woodworking teacher while she studied nursing at Knapp College of Nursing at Cottage Hospital in Santa Barbara. When they graduated they would marry. While a student, Nick helped with search and rescue for the San Franscisquito Dam Disaster in Newhall.

The Depression hit the economy just as he was ready to graduate. Of the two hundred students in his graduating class, only three found jobs. He resisted farming; crop prices had fallen below the cost of producing them. He leased his land for what he could get and struggled to find work. After several years of temporary jobs, including that of a furniture salesman for Sarah's uncle in Lynwood, Nick decided that he could make more money farming. In 1935, after several years' absence, he moved back to the Conejo. The old home place, his childhood home, now belonged to his brother Lud's stepson. He rented the house and settled into farming.

In 1947, Lud's stepson decided to move back to the property. Nick, Sarah and their four children had to build a new house on their own land. They chose the saddle of a hill that overlooked the colony, at the northeast corner of Moorpark and Olsen Roads. The cost of materials in the post-war building boom was prohibitive for a cash-strapped farmer. Nick used lumber from the old *Wuthering Heights* movie set that had been filmed in the Norwegian Colony in 1938. He managed to scrounge and barter for a variety of new and used materials like the hardwood flooring that came from the stage/gym of the old Pleasant Valley School in Camarillo. The house cost $7,000 and took the family two years to build.

Eventually, Nick took a position as head of the furniture/woodshop department with the Camarillo State Hospital and worked there until his retirement. Sarah worked as a nurse at the State Hospital, progressing up the ranks to senior psychiatric supervisor.

Through years of juggling economic survival with his passion for knowledge, Nick developed into a master builder. He made 1/32 scale ships as a hobby, and made a half-size stagecoach that he later donated to the Stagecoach Inn Museum where it is on permanent display. He was active in Sons of Norway. He traveled to Norway five times, first with Sarah, who died in 1972, and, later, with his second wife, Jenni. Through his encouragement, several of our Norwegian second and third cousins have visited California.

Uncle Nick seemed sophisticated and urbane when compared with Grandpa. Many years separated the two in age. Grandpa had been Ellen and Nil's third child; Nick, had been their tenth and youngest. Each possessed native intelligence and natural curiosity that allowed them to be lifelong learners. For each of them, life took unpredictable turns that could have made them bitter, but they changed their course with positive attitudes.

Father and sons seemed plagued by mischance. Grandpa had been set to go off to engineering college when his father lost three fingers greasing the gears of a windmill. Weary from a lifetime of farming, wanting an easier life for his ailing wife, Nils retired to Moorpark and divided his holdings between his sons. Grandpa curtailed his engineering plans because he was needed on the farm. Nick had prepared himself for a career in education. Fate conspired to keep the brothers living within sight of each other for most of their lives.

In time, Nick and Oscar, outlived the pastoral ambiance of their valley. In 1955, as old men, they gathered in the little Olsen cemetery to identify the remains of their brother and sisters while the County Coroner instructed a backhoe driver to unearth the broken bits of fifteen wooden coffins, seven of them child-sized.

When the graveyard was unearthed, Nora's coffin was found to be perfectly preserved, as solid as the day Nils finished it. Inside, her mother's handpicked posies were still intact, dried in bunches at the child's head and feet.

Someone snapped a photo of Grandpa watching the unearthing. Sadness lined his worn face. The unblemished coffin had accomplished for him what forty years of grieving hadn't; his eyes clouded with tears. The photo, like his childhood remembrance card, seemed to belong in a bureau drawer, out of sight. It was placed into an album and not shared until after his death.

The children's remains were combined into a single metal coffin and re-interred in the Ivy Lawn Memorial park in Montalvo. A placard with their names marks their resting-place. The brothers purchased a second casket for the hired men: Martin, run over by a hay wagon; and George Ness, who shot himself with his own gun under questionable circumstances.

Ness shot himself in 1911. Although the newspaper reported that it was the result of a gun-cleaning incident, conjecture clouded the incident. Ness had recently returned from the Klondike, despondent and ill. He died in his relative's small house, apparently busy cleaning his gun while the others were outside trying to round up a neighbor's herd of cows foraging in their grain field. The act seemed illogical to those that knew the truth.

It was said that his tombstone never stood upright. Each time the Olsens visited the graveyard, his stone would be tipped onto its side and they would set it upright again and dig it into the adobe soil. The next time they visited, it would be tilted again.

The cemetery unearthing seemed an apt ending to an era of history. Grandpa and Uncle Nick united in brotherly camaraderie as they bade their final farewells.

Anne Schroeder

Chapter Five
Coming Together

For a farmer, silence—or its close companion, stillness—rates high on his list of necessities. A half century before my great-grandfathers arrived in Southern California, other men abandoned field and farm in search of stillness when their Ohio or Pennsylvania forests began ringing with the sound of other men's axes. They loaded their families into Conestoga wagons, hitched farm animals to the yoke and journeyed to ever-distant lands. When the Pacific Ocean bounded the western horizon, many of them settled in Oregon and California. Some, perhaps, made it to the Conejo.

My grandfather's father was born in Norway. The family home still perches on a narrow shelf beside the Störfjord. It remains a solitary house with only a rowboat or mail boat for access. A generation or two earlier the house stood a hundred feet further west, until an overhead cliff broke off and an avalanche covered house and its inhabitants with rubble. The survivors built a new house and continued with their lives.

They derived their income from the sale of candy to a shop in town and from the herd of goats that grazed the steep cliffs. When summer ripened the grass on the plains above, the most agile family members climbed ropes to the top, gathered and sheathed the grass, and lowered it by ropes to be stored for winter fodder in the top story of the house.

Nils saved his fare and immigrated to California. To get the money for passage, $58, he saved for two years after he got out of the Norwegian Navy.

My grandfather seemed to seek stillness. It integrated his parts, rendered him complete. Like his father before him, he needed the solitude to process his reasoning and logic. Whenever confounded, Grandpa would leave the warmth of hearth and kitchen and walk the hills or the cow paths. In the quietness of nature, his

43

internal process blotted out the cacophony of modern life. When angered, he would leave the room and work among his animals or his machinery until his nerves calmed. He carried his opinions until he saw a reason to change, which could be years. He could forgive the sinner, but never the sin. In its purest form, the silence of falling dusk was to his soul what the ring of a cash register is to the merchant, the hiss of foaming lager to a bar patron. For Grandpa, silence served as a reminder that life is good.

From childhood I observed that the farmers of my acquaintance seemed not opposed to conversation so much as satisfied with the good, natural conversations that they carried on inside their heads during a lifetime of solitary labor. A gregarious farmer might talk to his dogs or, for lack of other companionship, to his sheep and cattle.

If every farmer was like Grandpa, by the end of the day he had settled his conflicts. He could return to the house with no need to speak of matters that troubled him. When he gathered with other farmers, conversation was often in the form of information gathering and exchange. He would process it later, when solitude afforded the opportunity.

For the farmer's wife, solitude often carried a steeper price. When the Norwegians blasted a road that connected them to civilization, it came too late for the wives whose husbands died of typhus, and for Ellen Olsen, whose children died without access to a hospital.

When Lud Olsen stopped farming and moved to Santa Barbara it was because his wife could no longer tolerate the remoteness of the Colony. That he turned to drink, divorced some years later and died of stomach cancer at a young age might suggest that he had abandoned the enterprise that made him whole.

The land was our heritage, a bond to the past when Great-great grandfather Caspar Borchard, Sr. traveled from a small town in Germany to buy a farm. He worked as hard as it took to thrive. At the Stagecoach Inn Museum, a docent tells the story that when Caspar's first wife died, he returned to his hometown in Germany, stood on a tavern table and announced, "I'm rich. I'm from America. I'm looking for a wife. Do I have any takers?" Someone mentioned the offer to a relative, Theresa Maring. An arrangement was struck.

In point of fact, Caspar Borchard, Sr.'s path to the Conejo was a bit more circuitous and a lot less swashbuckling. His brother Christian had departed for California two years earlier and failed to send word home of his whereabouts. His well-to-do family in the city of Hanover, Germany, worried. Caspar, at twenty-two, faced conscription into the German army, and he decided that a trip to California was the better choice. He found his brother in Antioch, herding sheep.

After working for a time in Antioch, Caspar bought a thousand acres near Oxnard, but had some difficulty transferring the funds to pay for it. He decided that he must return to Germany to attend to the details. While waiting to board his ship, he was invited by a stranger to have a drink. Not accustomed to strong spirits, he found his new friend pressing one drink after another on him as he tried unsuccessfully to decline. Upon leaving the bar he tripped (or was struck) and awoke to find his wad of money missing from his waistcoat.

With his passage money gone, the boat sailed without him. He was forced to forfeit the land purchase and to return to Antioch to work for new passage money home. A few years later he sailed again for Germany.

When he returned to America, he rented land in Ventura County and farmed for three years.

After arranging for his brother to farm the land until he could purchase it, Caspar sailed to Germany for a wife. There he married Theresa, a delicate woman of uncertain health. As he was packing to return to California, her parents prevailed upon him to put off the trip until their daughter's health improved. Unwilling to see his in-laws suffer, he agreed. Instead of improving, his bride declined steadily. Three years later she died.

Like Jacob and Rachel in the Old Testament, Caspar bided his time until he could return to his chosen land. He buried his wife, waited through a one-year mourning period then married a second Theresa, a neighbor named Theresa Maring. The following day they set sail for California.

With money in his pocket to purchase his land, he found his brother John and John's wife comfortably settled on his farm. They had expected to caretake for less than a year, but it had been over four years. Caspar could scarcely expect them to leave. Instead, he bought two hundred acres from Godfrey Maulhardt and farmed it for nine years.

In 1888, he, Theresa, and their children moved to the Conejo. He purchased his Conejo Ranch piecemeal: 3,115 acres from one man and 1,047 acres from another, for a total of $6,366, according to the deeds of sale. This works out to be $6.08 per acre.

The Ventura County Star Free Press reported on May 5, 1893, that Caspar Borchard, Sr. had built one of the largest barns in the county on the Conejo, measuring 72'x100'x36 1/2' high.

Theresa bore eight children. Her oldest girls were in their early twenties when she died at forty-nine of stomach cancer. Her death came unexpectedly. She was feeling poorly so her husband rushed her to a doctor's office in Ventura. The doctor examined her and determined that she needed to be hospitalized. After a day's rest at a relative's house in Ventura, she was reloaded into the back of Caspar's spring wagon, onto a mattress he had placed there for her comfort. When daylight arrived, he headed the buggy toward St. Vincent's Hospital in Los Angeles.

The cancer was too advanced. She returned home to die. Her children recalled that her last request, as they pressed against her deathbed, was that they "go to church all of their lives." To a one, they complied.

After her mother's death, Mary, the oldest girl, remained a spinster in order to raise her brothers and sisters: Rosa (twenty-two at the time), Leo, Caspar, Antone, Frank, Charles and Teresa, and to keep house for their father. In the family it was said (perhaps with romantic license) that she turned down an offer of marriage to devote her life to her siblings.

After the children married and had families of their own, Mary visited her nieces every week, bringing flowers and vegetables from her garden. Wednesday luncheons gave the hard-working women something to look forward to. The visits also provided the opportunity for the ladies to exchange family news. Because Nana was much older than her sisters, and her mother much older than hers, our line included the oldest daughters born of oldest daughters for several generations. While the men were out farming and the children playing in the yards, we sat at table and I learned to process information for subtleties, to listen for the unspoken clues.

Nana's daughter, Aunt Mary, became the keeper of the family flame. She understood the significance of family affairs and the value of family unity. Through her, Great Aunt Mary Borchard's weekly luncheons live on, in a sense.

My Great-grandmother Rosa seemed to me a stern, sensible woman, tall and thin, hale from a lifetime of hard work. Her husband, Silas, was a sociable, well-liked Irishman who spun the best yarns in the valley and worked like a dervish when the urge struck him. Undoubtedly Rosa was attracted to him. He had worked for her father on the Borchard Ranch so she knew him well by the time they were married in 1899, when she was twenty-three.

Rosa was born in New Jerusalem, the old name for El Rio, on the east-end of Oxnard. Later she attended Timber District School when classes were held in the Stagecoach Inn. After graduation she attended parochial school in Los Angeles while living with relatives in the area. Her father arranged that she travel to Hanover, Germany, to visit relatives before her marriage. She was a shy, quiet girl whose personality was replicated in my mother. Afraid of horses, she seemed to fear automobiles as well, and never learned to drive. Throughout her life, her children chauffeured her wherever she needed to go.

Silas was the son of John Reily Kelley, a dependable farmer who had proven his mettle to Caspar Borchard enough to believe that Silas would be a good son-in-law. "John Reily" was a good farmer, although his sons, for the most part, did not share his enthusiasm for farming.

When Silas failed to thrive as a farmer, Caspar's thinking centered on a single-minded solution to his son-in-law's economic woes: sheep could be run profitably in the crags and buckhorns of Silas' land where little else could thrive. But Silas was adamant in his hatred of sheep. For Caspar, Silas' refusal to consider sheep seemed to grind insult into the face of reason.

Other differences divided the two men. Caspar was a man driven by the need to acquire more and more land. Thrifty and long-sighted, he could see the benefits of hard work and sacrifice. In contrast, Silas was a sociable man. A true son of Ireland, he was a storyteller. People gravitated to him because his blarney brought lighthearted relief to the serious business of living. In another era he might have made his fortune as a salesman. Instead he was destined to live out his life in the midst of a clan whose values he didn't wholeheartedly embrace, and whose approval he couldn't earn.

During the 1920s, his fondness for "demon rum" created discord between Silas and his wife's family, but his most intolerable character flaw seemed to be that he didn't want to farm.

Rosa remained loyal to her husband. Probably she could see both sides of the argument and seemed determined to suffer in silence. She said little, even when Silas frequently strayed off to a speakeasy and left her alone with the children. She would not have been comfortable in the low lights of a tavern, but it was in the presence of lubricious companionship that Silas flourished. When he occasionally disappeared for a week at a time, always at the end of harvesting season, Rosa pursed her lips and spent her days among her chickens and turkeys until he returned. Everyone who knew her agreed; she turned to her garden and her chickens and left her husband to his follies.

It must have put Rosa in an untenable position, living within sight of her father and having to listen to his opinions. There was little privacy for the couple to settle their marital differences. When Silas failed to return home after a night of merry-making, his absence was obvious. When his car was missing from its usual parking spot, Rosa's brothers knew to drop by to milk the cows and feed the pigs.

Silas was an inordinately popular man and his children took pride in him. They didn't allow tales to be carried about his exploits. He was their father, and they were proud of their birthright.

His sons understood their father and enjoyed his company. They drove him to speakeasies, drank alongside him, and in the wee hours of the morning brought him home again, happy and inebriated and probably in trouble with their mother.

It was Silas' damnable luck that Ventura County, at the turn of the century, became a seedbed for the Temperance Movement. Photographs of determined women wielding hatchets made front-page news. While Silas and his sons hauled bootleg whiskey out the backdoor of a distiller's house in Thousand Oaks, Temperance ladies might burst through the front door, intent on emptying unconsumed inventory onto the streets. In this atmosphere, Silas' habits were noted among his neighbors. He might have seemed flamboyant in the conservative era. Today his behavior probably wouldn't raise an eyebrow.

Silas Kelley worked as hard as any farmer of the era. It wasn't reputation as a worker that put him at odds with his in-laws. For Caspar, Sr., it was worse than that. When his father, John Reily, passed away, Silas sold his birthright.

"You never sell land," Caspar Borchard, Sr. fretted. "You only buy land." He was afraid that if he left Rosa her share, Silas would sell that, too, and lose the proceeds in some ill-conceived investment. In 1913, Caspar, by then a widower, wrote a will that bypassed his son-in-law and left Rosa's share to her children with a rider guaranteeing her life estate. The next year he revised the will to include a provision that the children provide financial support for their mother until her death with the income from their inherited land.

The plan worked, more or less. Rosa's sons contributed to her upkeep. She lived with frugality, and her offspring learned never to entrust our support to our children.

When Silas died in 1929, she had been married to him for thirty years. She lived another thirty years as his widow. As she grew older, she assumed a weariness that defined her as it did many of the women of her era. Into her late seventies she still found the will to maintain a garden and her hen house, hang her wash, and keep a spotless house. Like her sisters, fate graced her with a long life. She lived well into her eighties.

In 1910, the first automobile traveled through the Conejo. In 1914, Silas bought one of the first in the valley. He liked any excuse to run errands for his neighbors. In the late 1920s, opportunity took him off the ranch when he was hired by the Ventura County Public Works Department as construction foreman to supervise the paving of public roads. He excelled at this job. He knew how to work with people and his reputation was that of a fair and enthusiastic boss. His career came to an end when his position—a political plum—was coveted by a more politically connected rancher. Silas was dismissed without cause and without a pension.

Earlier in the decade he had formed a short-lived partnership with a young man named Louie Goble. Louie had left a privileged life in New York to join the circus and found himself in Los Angeles when the circus wintered there. For a period of time he worked at Universal Studios, cleaning up after the animals until Universal eliminated their wild animal zoo—and with it, his job. He purchased some land in Thousand Oaks and brought with him his two lions, Pasha and Queenie. Pasha was the original MGM lion until Leo took his place.

Louie owned the lions; Silas owned the truck. Silas traveled around the countryside buying up old or crippled horses for the lions to eat. It was through this connection that he eventually rescued one and brought it to Nana so his granddaughters could have their own pony.

Louie wanted to get another lion in order to establish a breeding farm in Thousand Oaks, but he lacked the money. He had spent all of his savings, $50, for five lots in the new subdivision of Thousand Oaks. He formed an equal partnership with Silas Kelley—who neglected to discuss the matter with his wife, and failed to mentions his intentions to travel with the exhibit until the loan was repaid. Rosa wasn't keen on the idea when she found out. When Louie was able to come up with the money, he bought out Silas' share.

The Lion Farm became a fixture in Thousand Oaks. Some claim that it built the town, gave people a reason to seek out the dusty burg with its profusion of live oak trees and predictably balmy weather.

As Louie's finances and reputation grew, he branched out into other exotic animals, trained and leased them to the movie industry, and changed the Lion Farm's name to The Jungle Compound. In the 1950s it was sold and renamed

Jungleland. Among our family, it was always referred to as the Lion Farm, even when camels spat at us over wire fences and trumpeting elephants broke the silence of the night.

Rose, Dorothy (holding lion cub), Babe, and Josephine and Babe's childern, Catherine and Johnny. Ca.1930.

Whatever its name, The Lion Farm was a hard neighbor to ignore. In the '40s, roaring lions could be heard from eight miles away, all the way to the Norwegian Colony.

From time to time, an animal escaped captivity. Most were recaptured, but a black panther lived out its life in the hills behind Newbury Park, to the consternation of local citizens.

As his fortunes grew, Louie Goble built a commercial front to his compound, a cluster of buildings that housed a fire department and a burgeoning business center.

Nana's sister, Dorothy, attended beauty school in San Pedro and opened a beauty shop in one of Goble's units next to the fire department. As the family's first working woman, she gave her nieces "Shirley Temple" perms and shared Conejo news with her stay-at-home sisters when they dropped by to visit. After she married, she closed up shop for a year to follow her husband to Long Beach during World War II. When her husband shipped out on the USS Oklahoma to Pearl Harbor, she returned and reopened the shop.

On the day that the Japanese bombed the harbor and the Oklahoma was sunk, Nana and her brother, Fred, and their families heard the news on the radio. They invented an excuse to spend the afternoon with Dorothy in case she received bad news. They had agreed ahead of time that no one would tell her about the bombing until after dinner. Over a half century later, Fred's son, Freddie remembers that he blurted it out in the middle of supper. His Aunt Dorothy had to be revived from a swoon and he received the bawling-out of his life.

Dorothy was forced to wait for over two months for a message that her husband was safe. When his letter arrived, heavily censored, he explained that he had been briefly hospitalized with injuries incurred when he jumped over the side of the battleship. With characteristic good fortune that would follow him through his life, he had landed in a lifeboat.

Chapter Six
Irish Laughter,
Irish Tears

The members of Grandpa Olsen's family were non-drinkers, sober, industrious people who squeezed a full day's work out of their waking hours. Above all else, this seemed to be what Nana valued in a mate. Her mother's experience had imbued in her distrust for fraternizing men. When she looked around for a husband, the admonition that "he drinks" was enough to dismiss a young man from consideration.

Grandpa fit her criteria. He held to his promise never to take a drink. We substituted tea, hot and iced, and Watkins orange concentrate, and lemonade made from lemons picked from Nana's front yard.

My mother passed this attitude onto her own children. In her and Nana's eyes, how much or how little a man consumed wasn't the point. A drinking man was not to be considered. Like Nana's father, a drinking man had the potential to lie dormant for many months before his habit exploded—when his pockets were filled with cash from the sale of summer beef.

Nana's brothers' exploits were legendary. They raced horses—and later, model T's and roadsters. They stayed out late, caroused on Saturday nights and managed to ruffle the feathers of their reserved aunts and uncles up the road. Great-uncle Ed Borchard was not amused when a couple of his Kelley nephews cut the tip off of his cigar, filled it with dirt, and fastened the tip back on. They watched as he tried, unsuccessfully, to get a draw.

In the Irish tradition, the Kelley children were numerous. Charlie, a quiet man who never married. He subscribed to the Los Angeles Times and let his nephews read the Sunday funnies. He was drafted into World War I, but escaped service when the war ended while he was still in training camp. Theresa was serious, thrifty, my grandmother. John balanced his Irish with his German ancestry. Walter was garrulous, and childless, until his wife, Helga, had a grown son show up at her doorstep whom she had neglected to tell him about. Fred, the youngest boy, was smart, social and easy going, the Fire Captain at Port Hueneme. Rose, a pretty girl, died of breast cancer at thirty-six. Dorothy, a shy girl, married a Cajun man that her cousin met at a cockfight, and Josephine, ebony-haired and Irish fey, was the vivacious youngest.

The siblings ages spanned so many years that the two younger girls, Dorothy and Josephine, had their babies at the same time as my mother, their niece. The result was an assortment of first and second cousins that created confusion for outsiders, including our teachers at Timber School where four generations of Borchards attended through the years.

We children understood the difference between a first and a second cousin. The distinction affected the parties that we were invited to, the gossip that we were privy to. At Christmas time, when no single house could contain all of us, we second cousins dropped in at Grandma Kelley's for a few minutes, after her grandchildren opened their gifts. Grandma always had a plastic stocking filled with candy and oranges for each of us.

Regardless of the fact that we celebrated our big Christmas the following night, I always envied the Kelley cousins. My mother reminded us that we had another set of first cousins and they had only each other.

Growing up among Kelleys and Borchards, I envied those who carried the family name. My father's name, Thompson, seemed plain. It obscured my claim to Kellyness. I wondered how Nana felt when she changed her name to Olsen.

Family names were used and reused. If babies weren't christened with their aunt's or uncle's first names, they often carried them as a middle name: Margaret, Theresa, John, Edward. To avoid confusion, duplicates were referred to by their last name: Theresa Maulhart, Teresa Borchard, (the 'h' was dropped because it had been used for an older sister who died at birth. Anyway, we called her "Aunt Tracy". Theresa Olsen (Nana was called Tracy), and me. We had difficulty ourselves distinguishing between Margaret Borchard, Margaret Borchard Bartel, and Edward and Margaret Borchard—all different Margarets, all different Borchards. A name was a way of tying the generations together, of honoring both the newborn and the original. My mother offended Nana by dropping the 'h' in my first name, Teresa, and insisting that I be called by my middle name. In the family, it was a breach of tradition.

Nana's brothers probably thought she was dour. She possessed a serious, critical side, but the Kelley siblings were heart-and-soul involved in each other's lives. The Borchards and Kelleys, especially the first cousins born in the decades of the twenties and thirties, were fortunate. The isolation of the Conejo forced them to share almost every facet of their lives and bred a tribe of cousins almost sibling-like in closeness.

My Uncle Neil was the exception. Shy like his Norwegian father, his visits to the Kelley clan were fraught with the same practical jokes and teasing that his father had endured a generation earlier. Neil stayed at his Grandmother Kelley's house on only three occasions. As a boy he had to stick close to the house when-ever he visited because Nana wanted him to avoid his cousins' bad influences. He had little in common with his Irish cousins, didn't inherit their jovial outlook. Reared into his father's habit of hard work, at sixteen he was already doing a man's work. He leased pasture from his father, and he raised sheep and grain to earn his college tuition. From his father, he learned to haggle prices with the Jewish cattle buyer who came at daybreak on Sundays. Even if he wished, he had little time to recreate with his Kelley cousins.

When, as old people, the Kelleys spoke of the early days their recollections were peppered with stories of each other. Those listening would nod their heads in agreement. As the younger generation listened, they understood that their lives were an extension of their parents'. The two generations were connected. The fact that some members weren't born until twenty-five years later didn't temper their appreciation for the stories. In spirit they were there. In spirit they still are.

When I look at group photographs taken at family reunions, I recognize over a hundred faces. Memories and emotions connect me to most of them. Those people affected me even as a child, plain-faced folks with booming laughter and a penchant for long-winded stories.

Through my mother, I inherited a mix of Irish and Norwegian disposition. Even as a child, I was grateful for the Irish side, for the way that my great-uncles and uncles-in-law livened up our huge family picnics. Red-faced and garrulous after a few trips to their trucks, they could be counted on to hire a bagpiper and dance a jig. When they told their stories, we children sat nearby and tried to pretend that we weren't listening so that our mothers wouldn't whisk us away.

Celebrations were always held outdoors with picnic tables made of sawhors-es and barn planks. The were piled high with food, including Grandma Kelley's famous German potato salad. In the early years, the tables were set up in her yard, (now called Rosa Lane) beneath a huge live oak and a towering *Washingtonia* palm tree. As the family grew, the party moved to Oak Grove Park at the base of the Conejo Grade and opened up to all the family, a hundred and fifty or more Borchards and Kelleys, Freidrichs and Olsens, Colwells and Ashbys. Hardly anyone traveled more than twenty miles to attend.

Great-uncle Walter would lead some of the fellows on surreptitious trips to the front seat of his battered green pickup, after which the tempo of the party would pick up. Usually he offered my sisters and me a quarter to sing a pretty song. He usually requested "You Are My Sunshine", which we sang in three-part harmony while we avoided our mother's frown. Mama felt we should refuse the money, offered as it was by an inebriated man. In her opinion, Walter offered a poor example. One year he got boisterous and engaged his brother in a wrestling match. The two middle-aged men butted and backed each other to the ground while we children watched with saucer-sized eyes.

Walter loved a good party, but within the family he was the keeper of the flame. When his sister, Rose, traveled to Ashland, Oregon in search of a cure for cancer, Walter went along and cared for her. He kept up her spirits and relayed news from the family while he sought treatment for his asthma.

Rose's husband, Harry Fletcher, stayed behind to work and to care for the children, including baby Patrick, barely weaned when his mother was stricken.

Tragedy had already struck Rose's family. Two years earlier, a panther fatally clawed her two-year-old son, Donnie, when she was three months pregnant with Patrick. The panther, a pet of their neighbors, the Louie Gobles, was chained on a vacant lot. The neighborhood children often played with it. Donnie was returning from his grandmother's, two houses down, with a cookie in his hands. He put the cookie in his mouth as he tried apparently to pet the panther, and it swiped the cookie, tearing his throat with its sharp claws.

His father, Harry, drove him to St. John's Hospital in Oxnard while his mother cradled him in her arms. Three days later he died. He was buried on his second birthday.

Six months later, Patrick was born. A few months after that, Rose was diagnosed with cancer.

After Rose's death, Harry eventually married Olga, a widow with a son, Sandy, from a previous marriage. Harry and Olga, Sandy, and Rose's sons, Ralph and Patrick lived in Thousand Oaks for several years and then built a home on Rose's land.

Olga seemed to resent the forced association with the Kelley clan. One of her sisters-in-law recalls her returning a Christmas gift unopened. It was a shirt that had been given to Patrick by his aunt, a Kelley. Rose's boys could not accept a gift unless Olga's son received one as well.

Harry died first. When Olga passed away, her will designated her entire estate to Sandy. Rose's sons got none of their mother's land.

Walter cared for another sister, Dorothy, while she lay dying of cancer in the City of Hope Hospital in Los Angeles. He stayed in a boarding house connected with the hospital. Her family visited regularly, but he remained at her side until she died so that she wouldn't be alone.

In happier times, the Kelley boys told ear-popping stories about people that we all knew. They knew how the great men came upon their fortunes, or lost their fortunes, or got bucked off a cantankerous horse into the cactus. At family picnics, the gathering centered at the table where the three Kelley brothers sat.

Sometimes they would decide to drive home, would try to climb into their cars until someone took their keys. Their brand of humor was hearty. In a crowd of people, a Kelley, brother or sister, could be recognized by the sound of their laughter. I thought my great-aunts and uncles were wonderful.

By the early 1950s, when I knew them, it was a rare occasion when one of the Kelley boys forgot their manners under the influence of strong spirits. Silas had died of heart trouble, his son, Charlie, of a heart attack, and the others had mellowed with age.

Charlie had been an alcoholic, but he took "the cure" in his thirties and never drank again. Quiet, non-complaining, he worked for the Janss Ranch and usually got assigned the dangerous jobs that none of the married men wanted.

After he retired from the Janss Ranch, Charlie worked as a maintenance man for Ventura County. At work, he spent his last day crawling inside huge tanks and cleaning them out with carbon tetra-chloride. Later that night he suffered a fatal heart attack. It wasn't until years later, when others suffered the same fate, that doctors made a connection between the chemical and his heart attack.

Uncle Fred was moderate in manner. He was in charge of the fire department at Port Hueneme Naval Base. He was also the last surviving Kelley brother on the Conejo. Intelligent and quiet-spoken, he lacked the flamboyance of his brothers, but his intelligence was his bequest to his children and grandchildren. Two of his sons, Billy and Fred, Jr. continue to live in the Conejo.

Uncle John, my grandmother's twin, inherited his father's charm and gift of storytelling. His wife, Babe, kept him on the straight and narrow. He enjoyed a

Anne Schroeder

Grandpa and Nana stood up for John and Babe on their wedding day in 1923.

certain amount of drinking and levity, but he usually called it a night when he got a signal from Babe. We children loved him. He was handsome, kind and clever, a magnet for friends. He imbued every gathering with a sense of fun. Photos of him as a young man show a slim, self-assured man with the Western actor, Sam Elliott's, dark eyes. He and Nana and Grandpa stood up for each other at their weddings and were close of all their lives.

Years later, knowing that twins skipped a generation, it was my fondest hope that I would produce the next set, but that honor was bestowed on my younger brother Matt, a dead ringer for Uncle John.

Aunt Babe and Uncle John married two years after Nana, as soon as Babe finished high school. Her name was Olive, although only her teachers called her that. The rest of us called her "Babe", the nickname given her by her father on the day of her birth. Babe empowered me before I knew what the word meant.

Her mother had been married to a man who left for long periods to hunt for gold in the Klondike. When gold eluded him, he earned his living toting equipment and supplies, a hundred pounds at a time, on his back, over the daunting Chilcoot Trail. After an absence of seven years he returned to his wife, who had no inkling of whether he was alive or not. She declared that if he ever left again, she would divorce him. He did and, true to her word, she did.

Babe's father was a butcher who did contract butchering for Caspar Borchard, Sr. He met Babe's mother when he rode his bicycle from Hueneme to Hollywood to buy lemons from her citrus orchard. Either he had heard about the pretty widow or he had a terrific yen for lemons.

When Babe's mother died of cancer, her father fostered her out to a Mexican family with eight children. She loved being a part of a big family. When one of the younger girls got pregnant, Babe's father decided that it wasn't a fit environment for his daughter and placed her with a childless, older couple who doted on

56

her until she married.

Photographs of Babe as a young girl show a self-assured, athletic girl who loved tennis. She was a member of California's first Girl Scout troop which Julia Lowe, the founder of the Girl Scouts, visited when she came west. Babe raised three fiercely independent children, all high achievers. She sent her daughter, Catherine, to the University of California at Los Angeles. My mother called Babe "a woman ahead of her time".

Great-uncle John and Babe, farmer and housewife, seemed more sophisticated than the rest of the family. When one of their children grew up to become a veterinarian with photographic memory, another an U.S. State Department translator and international educator, their success seemed to validate us.

It was so with Great-uncle Fred, whose son, Fred, Jr., earned his engineering degree at U.C. Berkeley and traveled the world as an engineer. But he served his apprenticeship at his Uncle Walter's dairy. At age seven he learned to drive Walter's hay truck. After his eighth birthday, he milked eighteen cows on the weekends when Walter's regular milker had time off. Three milkings a day, eighteen cows per milking; he was eight years old. For this he earned seventy-five cents for the weekend. After the morning milking he helped run the bottled milk route. With his Uncle Walter, he hauled five and ten gallon cans of milk to the creamery in Ventura. After the afternoon milking, he bottled milk and separated cream.

When his brother, Bill, turned eight, he started milking, too.

Fred, Jr.'s son graduated with an M.D. in bio-medical physics and maintains a career in Public Health. Presumably he knows how to milk a cow.

When I attended college, education had become the accepted reward for an intelligent young mind. Any son or daughter of a farmer that pursued higher education seemed to be escaping a life of mindless toil. But looking back, I failed to understand another version of this history lesson.

Before the era of child labor laws, work was the way that families bonded. With the advent of labor laws, physical work has been relegated to the undereducated, and its value has been denigrated as something to be avoided by anyone with intelligence. We have broken our ties with the soil, to our detriment as a society.

I learned a valuable lesson watching the family at work and at play; whether labors are physical or mental, lives are wasted when a person fails to find his passion. If that passion is farming, so be it. If he or she is unable to follow his

Muse, like Silas Kelley, then his universe is interrupted and chaotic. In the days when travel was difficult, cash was scarce and Social Security did not provide retirement security, not everyone was able to follow their bliss.

Grandpa Olsen traveled to Los Angeles, as reported in the Moorpark Enterprise in 1916, "seeking to fit himself for engineering". Fate intervened: his father lost three fingers while oiling a windmill, retired from farming and divided his land between his three sons. Grandpa was nineteen when he began farming full-time. Before that, he managed nearly two years of high school, staying with a family in Ventura on the weekdays and returning home on the weekends. In later years he took classes at Moorpark High School night school, metals and wood-working.

His 1906 Webster's Dictionary is dog-eared, probably from the serious work of learning English as a second language. For his entire life he maintained a journal, noting weather and soil conditions, daily events and his own philosophical notes.

His farming was methodical, innovative, and thrifty. He kept bees to pollinate his citrus and apricot trees, and sold honey under his own label. He tore down his former school in Moorpark and used the lumber to build houses for his daughters when they married.

In the evenings when work was finished, he used his lathe to turn apricot limbs into candlesticks and bowls. After he retired, he built cherrywood jewelry boxes for each of his daughters and granddaughters, and bureaus and hutches to hold their dishes. In my fifteenth year, he spent months building me a piece of furniture that we designed together, an oak hutch with a pull-out desk and deep shelves behind glass doors to hold my books and doll collection.

He taught his grandchildren to collect stamps, coins, and rocks, and sat beside us as we acquired his habit of quiet concentration.

His mail contained more subscription magazines than I have seen collected in any one place except a library. He and Nana read them all and passed them on. They instilled in us a lifelong love of reading.

They never bought us a toy that I can recall. For Christmas presents, they gave books. I received *Olaf and Anne, Children of Norway; the Great Journey of Marquette and Jolliette;* and *Calling All Girls*, a monthly magazine of short stories, renewed for five Christmases. For high school graduation, I got *The Anthology of World Literature in Digest Form*. My grandparents understood their grandchildren's needs better than we did.

Grandpa taught us to value tradition. Each Christmas he handed out boxes of chocolate-covered cherries that he purchased from Sprouse-Reitz. Some of us loved the candy, some of us hated it, but the memory of this simple pleasure is a tender blessing. He was not a man given to endearments. When I learned that he courted Nana with a sack of chocolate-covered cherries, his gift seemed even more precious.

Before he inherited his land, Grandpa had just about taken the cure for farming. As a young man he would get up at 5:00 a.m., feed and harness the horses, milk the cow, eat breakfast and be out in the field by daybreak. At the age of seventeen, he decided that his father was unduly harsh so he determined to hire on with a neighbor, Mr. Lepeyre, for cash money. He was hired in due course, room and board included. His job was to get up at 5:00 a.m. to feed and harness the horses, milk the cow, eat breakfast and be out in the field by daybreak. But at Lepeyre's he had an additional chore. Mrs. Lepeyre was sick and her husband decided that his new hired man should baby-sit the children as he worked in the field.

Grandpa didn't think that a grown man should have to baby-sit and he liked his mother's cooking better. After a week he quit and returned home. He didn't have the nerve to knock at the door so he stood outside in the gathering dusk, wondering what to do. When his father passed by with the pail of milk, he glanced over, saw his son and said, "Better hurry. It's almost dinnertime." Neither of them ever again discussed the subject of his hiring out. Grandpa always thought that his father had set it up with Lepeyre to have him work just as hard as he did at home, but he couldn't bring himself to ask.

Chapter Seven
Lessons Learned

Among my cousins, many fifth-generation Borchards remain connected to the land. They have chosen careers as managers of corporate farms, as foremen of ranches like the Wood Ranch in Simi, as agricultural chemical spray experts, as nutritionists. They are professionals whose work reflects their farm roots.

Some cousins and uncles were fortunate enough to inherit land from their parents, to continue farming with an unbroken seam. When they took over control of their family farms, they did so as graduates of an agricultural college.

Today, college is an essential part of agriculture. Sons come home from college and argue progressive methods with their fathers the way that Caspar, Sr. and Silas Kelley argued about sheep. Their success will be more elusive than it was for our great-grandparents, who lived in the brief period of American farming when land was cheap, labor was plentiful and a burgeoning population paid well for crops that could not be shipped long distances. Caspar Borchard, Sr. and his neighbors made use of apprenticeship, common sense, and shared knowledge. Their great-grandsons use computers, accountants and genetic technology. If they could have a conversation with the old men of the Conejo, the present day farmers could undoubtedly hold their own.

The sound of Irish argument still stirs the evening breeze along Borchard Road. If one hears voices of old farmers raised in passionate discourse, it might be the Borchard or the Kelley brothers gathered around a celestial dinner table. The luxury of being able to strongly disagree belongs to families who know each other well.

Our ancestors might have applauded our flocking to the cities to earn university credentials, but they might be disappointed in our children's lack of common sense. Farm children have had to find their place in a society that no longer values their efforts. This task is made harder when they fail to realize the significance of education to increase their choices.

Whenever he was distracted from the classroom by the lure of a sunny day, Uncle Neil remembers being sent out to hoe weeds with the janitor. His teacher told him that he was only going to be a farmer, and he wouldn't need as much education as a town boy. That he was a hands-on learner didn't carry weight in the classroom.

When he was ten years old, he began rebuilding the engine on his father's worn out Studebaker. It took him two years, but as soon as it ran again, he drove it using a block for a driver's seat so he could see over the steering wheel. His early teachers were both right and wrong; he farmed his way through California Polytechnic College.

Farmers have traditionally held city people suspect until they show that they possess logical thinking. My family was no exception. My grandfather would have found ridiculous those labels on plastic buckets warning that a child might drown in six inches of water. Grandpa showed us to stand back while he donned a beekeeper's veil and walked among his buzzing hives. He rarely emerged with a red welt. The bees knew him and allowed him to share their world. "Use your head," he used to tell us. "That's what it's for."

For him, the safety of his children depended on their learning where danger lurked and how to avoid it. He taught his children to avoid the flywheels of tractors, irrigation ponds, rattlesnakes and overhead powerlines. The abstract was for thinkers, not doers.

Farmers like my grandfather were forced to invent, to reinvent, and to improvise in their surroundings to accommodate a cash-poor economy. Like most men of his profession, Grandpa prided himself on his self-sufficiency and his ability to master a situation. Like them, he shared his skills with anyone who asked.

Make-shift housing dotted the Conejo during the first part of the century. Single men lived in bunkhouses and almost everyone else lived on their farms. Few farmers could afford the expense of building a house that would last through the ages. Most houses were single-walled shacks, stud wall skeletons covered with wood siding that shrunk as it aged so that cold drafts blew through the cracks. Construction sheet rock didn't exist until after WW II. The thickness of a house was usually one layer of board. In the closets, two layers of wood provided a pocket into which a housewife could stuff newspapers to provide a crude insulation. The paper trapped disease-bearing dust. Rats and mice made their nests in the layers. When the odor became noticeable, walls and floors were sometimes taken up so that the newspapers could be replaced.

Housewives stretched cheesecloth or very thin muslin over interior stud walls and glued wallpaper onto the cloth with wheat flour paste. Housewives of that era complained that the walls flexed with every passing breeze.

Great-uncle John's first house was just such a shack, rented in what is now Wildwood Park. The door latch was broken and the landlord didn't see any need to fix it. John and Babe propped an Indian bowl against the door to keep it closed against snakes and skunks.

In their second house, in Ventu Park, Babe's aunt came to visit and watched in horror as several insects scuttled beneath a sheet of peeled-back wallpaper. She declared that the house was infested with bed bugs. Silas, Babe's father-in-law was present. Given to an outrageous sense of humor, he teased his young daughter-in-law by telling her that bedbugs would chew the ears off of her babies. Babe had a baby (her daughter, Catherine) in bed only inches from the wall.

Silas allowed that kerosene would kill most anything. Ignorant of its dangers, Babe sent Uncle John to Camarillo to pick up kerosene. When the guests departed, the two of them painted it onto the wallpaper, onto the floors, the attic and the doors. They poured some into small cans and set them beneath the baby's bed. Then they lit their kerosene lanterns and proceeded to go about their evening routine.

As an old lady, Babe still wonders at the miracle that they didn't burst into flame. She laughs today at her ignorance of most things domestic as a young bride in 1923.

Aunt Babe showed me the power of marching to one's own drumbeat. She was the catalyst in the family, the voice of reason, a laughing, spirited woman who didn't fit into any mold. She was not simply a farmer's wife, not just a housekeeper, but exciting and adventurous, a great talker, infinitely more young-at-heart than my other great-aunts. She was a disinterested cook who did so only when the urge struck. If Uncle John arrived home and no meal was ready, he cooked supper.

Uncle John, in the habit of the day, wore his hat everywhere. He was one of a generation of men with a white band across his forehead where his skin never met the sun. In later years, Babe liked to tell it that he wouldn't even answer the door without donning his hat.

Their oldest son, John, Jr. (Johnny) cowboyed for the Janss Ranch in the early 1950s. He later roped for the Hearsts, near present day Westlake Village. He was an amateur boxer in the El Rio boxing rings, a horseshoer, cowboy, roper and bull rider. He won All-Around Cowboy at the Ventura County Fair in 1949. His son, Nonnie, won the same award twenty years later.

One night he awoke, partially paralyzed. Even among his best friends, the stories differ. Some claimed that, as a cowboy, Johnny was tossed from his horse and injured his back. Some say that he injured his back picking up a horse trailer tongue. For four years he had experienced increasing pain as he worked as a horseshoer and pursued the rodeo circuit with an eye for a national title.

He was forced to choose between eventual, total paralysis or a risky back surgery. He elected for surgery in hopes that the damage could be corrected. It could not be. Johnny became resigned to the fact that he would be paralyzed. Through months of therapy, he saw slow improvement as the paralysis receded gradually from his neck down. Eventually he regained full motion of his arms and torso.

The community rallied to Johnny's aid with a fundraising barbecue arranged by his roping buddy, Fire Chief Tom Moody. Others came to his aid: his former bosses, dairywoman Belle Hollaway—for whom he had once hopped milk bottles—and Ralph Hays, his cousin, who owned Oxnard Plumbing and Roofing where Johnny worked as foreman. The population of the Conejo, at the time over 2,000 people, attended the barbecue and ate beef donated by Joel McCrea, the Borchard Brothers, and the Janss Corporation. The newspaper noted that everything was donated except the paper plates.

Johnny couldn't attend his party. Doctors wouldn't discharge him from the hospital for another three months. His friends and neighbors covered many of his medical expenses. More than that, they stayed his friends forever.

As a child I watched Johnny return from the Santa Monica Hospital and triumph over his despair. I watched his beautiful young wife, Alta, cope with grace and generosity over a situation that irretrievably altered her life.

When the despair lifted, Johnny began to salvage his options for a future that held little promise of the intense activity that he loved. For another year he continued therapy at his home. He designed a swimming pool, and his friends dug a pit in his front yard, framed it with wooden forms and re-bar, and poured a concrete swimming pool with a ramp at one end so that he could roll himself into the water. When he could drive again, he rigged a driving harness so that he could operate his station wagon.

When he was able to return to work, Johnny trained horses, rode fence lines, and brokered cattle and horses. He regained his sense of humor. Like his father, he regaled his listeners with the story behind every self-made rancher and big shot in the county. His storytelling was legendary.

Sometimes, instead of doing their homework, his sons gathered with his friends in their small living room and listened into the wee hours to his stories of the Conejo. His sons, Bill, Ralph and Nonnie were his legacy; they figured out the really important things in life before they got sidetracked.

Watching someone triumph over adversity was a gift from God. As children we absorbed lessons that I'm not sure Johnny knew he was teaching.

Dryland farmers and stockmen are a stoic breed. They can be identified from across a room. When a joke is told, sometimes the best they can manage is a "har har har", but the laughter doesn't quite fill their eyes.

When a herd bull gets tied up in barbed wire and has to be sold for slaughter, stockmen take out their frustration in a burst of hard work. They will go off by themselves for hours, maybe days, building fences or laying in a crop of hay while they try to make sense of their vulnerability. Maybe they don't recognize it as fear, but as a pervasive sense of fatalism, the way that things happen. Dryland farmers don't let themselves get too happy or too discouraged. It is their nature to hold something always in reserve.

When a dryland farmer looks out at his fields and sees a thick carpet of green poking through the sodden earth, he doesn't laugh at his good fortune. Too much can go wrong before the harvest. When his grain is knee-high and bowed with the weight of its barley heads, he casts an eye at the rainclouds and listens for thunder. He worries about a stray cigarette tossed out along the fenceline that borders the road. When the harvest is gathered into his granaries for the winter, he feels contentment in the year's efforts. He takes his wife to dinner, joins his neighbors at a dance and a potluck supper, talks yields and prices with his neighbors. He may take a day off to visit the county fair. Then he starts to worry about the coming year.

By the same measure, if grasshoppers eat his seed and the sun crusts the soil so that the seed can't germinate, if rains don't come and grass is half what he needs to hold his herd over the summer, he recalls the contentment of a full harvest. The memory keeps him going.

A farmer can't let himself get flat-out happy. He has already paid for the good times and he knows he will suffer the bad times again.

Stockmen are the same. They have too little control over their lives to be giddy. They settle for contentment in knowing that they live life on their own terms. It is a life that they wouldn't trade for anything on earth.

They seldom voice this feeling to outsiders and maybe not even to themselves. It is caught in the updrafts of air currents that stir the tree branches, in the cicadas that fly through the evening haze. The feeling resonates in the way that a man calls to his wife "Come quick," to share the 'v' flight pattern of mallards or geese flying south in the fall. Feeling the shared experience is as meaningful to the farmer as a bottle of vintage Chardonnay on a wine-seller's shelf.

When a child grows up surrounded by a family of dryland farmers, she can wonder if she was born without a gene that allows her to be outrageous. That was what Silas brought into the family. The Kelleys weren't so stoic. They didn't hold anything in reserve.

Chapter Eight
Sisters and Daughters

Silas Kelley died in the spring of 1929 and left Rosa with a life insurance policy. She deposited it along with her father's inheritance, a total of $10,000, in the Thousand Oaks Savings and Loan, an up-and-coming investment institution of the late twenties. Her sister Mary did the same with her inheritance.

When the stock market crashed later that year, the Savings and Loan went bankrupt. Rosa's family rallied around her, brought to their knees by the enormity of her losses. Letters, trips to the county seat, investigations did no good. The money had disappeared as surely as her hopes for a comfortable old age. The FDIC insurance program wasn't in effect in 1929. Investors were on their own.

For the rest of her life, Rosa Kelley lived with the sorrow of her failed investment. When her father, Caspar, died, the provisions of his will seemed to assure his grandchildren's lifetime support for Rosa. In later years, her sons and daughters disputed their obligation. Some of the more animated conversations at our family barbecues occurred between brothers and sisters who each didn't think that the other was paying a fair share.

While he lived, Charlie remained at home and provided his mother's support. After Charlie's death, Walter took over, farming his mother's land and paying her a sum for its use so that she had spending money.

By the 1950s, Rosa was in her 80s and needed live-in help, a fact that pressed home the question of support. Florence Hays, an area pioneer, was hired to care for Rosa. The children shared the cost.

Rosa's needs were simple; her family came first. She kept Silas' car, but she never learned to drive it. Her daughters or her daughters-in-law drove her wherever she needed to travel. When the car finally wore out she did not replace it.

Mary Borchard lost much of her cash after the crash as well, but she retained control of her land. She farmed her portion actively until her brother-in-law, Edward Borchard, assumed management after his marriage to her sister, Teresa. In my grandfather's records, I found a check made out in 1927 to Mary Borchard, for $7.50 for seed grain.

Aunt Mary remained with her father until his death. She kept house for the two of them in a two-story farm house that stood at the corner of what is now

Borchard Park, on Borchard Road. After her father's death, she moved in with Teresa and Edward.

There she cooked, sewed, and grew the oversized garden that supplied a hard-working farm family of three growing boys and two

Nana and sister Josephine on the Borchard Ranch, ca.1916

girls. Teresa never learned to sew, so Mary made the children's clothing, mended, and did the laundry.

Mary owned a '38 Packard and drove her two sisters on their errands. Extraordinarily thrifty and practical, she was probably wealthier than her brothers, yet she worked like a maid. She died a millionaire, but she cut down her old dresses to make her petticoats and underwear, and poured her strong coffee into a saucer to cool it before she slurped it from the saucer. Sharp-tongued and efficient, she was the work-worn saint of the family. Still, she seemed stern beside her gentle sisters, Teresa and Rosa. She sacrificed her life so that they might enjoy more gentile pleasures.

Aunt Mary was especially kind to my mother. When Mary moved from the old Borchard home she gave the huge, two-story farmhouse to my father for salvage. In doing so she bucked the advice of her brother-in-law, Edward, who wanted to sell the house for a goodly sum.

My father used the wood to build a small rental house on Charles Street in Moorpark, a washroom in our own house, and many cabinets and interior walls. Most of the boards were one-by-twelves sawn from old growth redwood, dense, clear, and often over twenty feet long.

The last time Aunt Mary drove, it was to visit my mother. She brought vegetables and cuttings from her garden and stayed for lunch. As she got into her car to drive the mile-and-a-half up the road to her house, she became confused and had to ask directions home. She never drove again.

Like her sister, she died in her late eighties, at Mary Health of the Sick Hospital, built on land that they had donated to the nuns.

During the mid-1950s, Nana received control of her inheritance, one hundred twenty-five acres of prime Conejo farmland. She kept the land in her name and handled her own finances. My sisters and I grew up understanding that men and women could have separate checking accounts, that sisters discussed taxes and real estate as well as hollyhocks and fruit preserves when they got together for afternoon tea. Her family respected Nana as much for her independent means as for her position as mother and grandmother. In the years before women's lib, her granddaughters watched and learned how things could be done.

Nana's discipline began early. After graduating from grammar school in 1914, she was able to attend high school in Oxnard for two years, commuting from the Conejo. Her brothers drove her to Oxnard to stay with friends, then returned for her on Friday afternoons so she could help her mother with weekend chores. Her report card for the years of 1915-16 showed: days absent, 0; days tardy, 0; straight 1's (the equivalent of A's).

After her marriage, Nana moved a few miles overland and settled in the brand new house that Oscar built for her on the west-end of the Norwegian Colony, on a farm with a seasonal creek and craggy bluffs where sheep could graze. It was a mail order house, purchased pre-cut for $2,500.00.

She and Grandpa traveled to Los Angeles to pick out the model, which she liked for its two bedrooms and built-in cabinets. When it came by train, Grandpa and his brother Nick drove two wagons to the train depot in Moorpark and loaded it for the trip back over the Norwegian Grade. The year was 1921.

Grandpa paid a Moorpark carpenter, Mr. Florey, $500 to help assemble the building. Each part had a number painted on it, and the men assembled the pieces like a huge jigsaw puzzle, complete with glass cabinets and bric-a-brac shelves. It gained attention as one of the finest houses in the area. Nana's mother was delighted for her. In later years Grandpa enclosed the porch and added two bedrooms to accommodate a growing family. But, from the first, it seemed perfect to Nana.

Nana's ways seemed as strange to her Norwegian in-laws as her Irish father's had been to his German in-laws. Ellen, Nana's mother-in-law, died two years after

Nana's marriage. Nana liked her and was saddened at her passing. Her neighbor, Karen Pederson, sometimes invited her to afternoon coffee with *krumkake* served on dainty cake plates, handmade doilies, and a coffee set that had been a wedding gift from Norway.

On the Colony, neighbors were few; young women such as Nana, even fewer. She never cared for her sister-in-law, Lud's wife, Hazel, a nervous woman who had little liking for the rural life. Eventually, her brother-in-law, Nick, married Sarah. Lawrence Pederson married Vida, and she gained a few neighbors. Most of the other Norwegians had long since left the Conejo.

Karn Pederson's Delicate Cake Recipe

1 cup butter, 2 cups sugar, 1 cup sweet milk, 3 cups flour, 5 eggs, whites only, 4 even teaspoons baking powder, flavor with lemon. No cooking time given.

Among her neighbors, Karen Pederson was famous for her cakes and cookies. Her granddaughter, Janet Reeling recalls Joel McCrea, the movie actor, visiting the kitchen when he dropped in to buy eggs. He had to duck his 6'6" frame under the door header and wipe his feet on the mat before he headed for the cookie larder. Karen would fetch a pitcher of milk and they would sit at the table and laugh and talk about the world.

After her marriage, Nana traded her horse for the ease of an automobile, although she rode occasionally, even into her forties. She liked horses better than Grandpa did, for riding, at least. Grandpa didn't trust them except for pulling wagons and farm equipment, and as soon as he was able, he replaced them with a tractor. He and his brother Lud were partners in an Overland automobile. It served both couples needs until each man could afford his own.

Nana spent her leisure time in her garden. Over the years she planted trees and roses, and flowers that attracted migrating butterflies on their way south to Mexico. Her garden was virtually identical to those of her mother and aunts. Her plants were starts from their gardens, carried as gifts for the hostess of their afternoon teas.

Before Nana and Grandpa married, Nils offered them the choice of his two farms. Grandpa was the second son and, as such, got second choice. He deferred to Nana. She chose the farm that Nils had purchased from George Hansen's widow. The rocky cliffs were picturesque and the terrain reminded her of Borchard Road. She picked a spot for her house behind the gum trees where she could neither see her neighbors nor be seen by them.

Grandpa's younger brother, Nick received the land that she didn't choose, Nils' original one hundred thirty-nine acres.

I imagine Nana as a bride, standing on the stoop of her brand new house, happy to be home. She didn't miss the rough-and-tumble days on the Kelley Ranch when her brothers occupied the bachelor wing of the upstairs farmhouse and clumped downstairs for dinner. She learned her skills cooking huge meals for cousins and hired men. In later years, her aunts told stories of how hard she worked, cooking and washing for everyone in the family.

As a sixteen-year-old, Nana ran the house for about a year, while her mother was being treated for breast cancer in Los Angeles.

After Rosa mentioned in a letter to her sister-in-law that she had developed a lump, her Los Angeles sisters-in-law arrived in their automobile, packed her up, and took her back to Los Angeles for treatment. Someone had told them of a woman who could cure cancer with a poultice that drew tumors from the body. They visited the woman at her home in Culver City and watched as she made a white poultice in a flannel wrap. She tied it under Grandma's arm, near her lymph gland. Within a period of months the poultice drew a growth with far-reaching roots—"feelers" as the woman referred to them—to the surface. Rosa returned home and lived to be eighty-five.

In later years the cancer story took on a sort of "wive's tale" element and was relegated to the we-won't-speak-of-it category. Fifty years later, my aunt, Mary Rydberg, was interviewing an old woman, Mrs. Miller, about her pioneer memories of Minnesota. Mrs. Miller mentioned that she had known a woman who cured cancer "with a poultice that drew the thing right out of the skin, feelers and all." Mrs. Miller claimed they lost touch when the healer moved to Los Angeles.

While her mother was gone, Nana held the fort at home. Her sisters were twelve, sixteen and eighteen years younger than she was and they weren't expected to work like Nana had done at their age. In later years, Grandpa often claimed that he married her to get her out of the house.

Nana's mother's first house, a thin-walled two-story, had been built by Rose's sister-in-law's father. Like in most farmhouses of the era, the ground floor was primarily kitchen and pantry. A built-in bench along one side of the table accommodated unexpected diners, the number of which varied with the harvest season. The bedrooms were small and unheated.

Later, a more modern house was built. It was smaller, but sounder, with two bedrooms and a parlor.

Behind the main house the men built a bunkhouse that became a haven for Nana's brothers and her cousins looking for independence from their fathers, and hired hands. The boys slept and played their guitars and lounged around with bachelor impunity, coming into the main house only for meals. Single men bunked at the ranch while they worked day jobs when they could find them, on harvesting crews, hoeing beans, or working sheep and cattle during the teens and 1920s. Uncle Walter, later used the bunkhouse to house his milkers when he operated his dairy.

The bunkhouse was strictly bachelor quarters. It was out of bounds to females. My mother remembers peeking inside, then running off before she could be caught and punished. The room was furnished with a solid row of beds and a straight back chair or two.

The Kelley boys lived in the bunkhouse for free. Others paid a token for board and room from their wages. Nana worked for no pay.

Fair womanhood seems to have engendered inequality among its Conejo maidens. To a startling degree, the ease of a woman's existence depended on the man she chose for her mate. Those who chose poorly served as a lesson to their nieces. The vagaries of fate courted some and teased others. Borchard women expected to live long lives. Many lived well into their eighties, with the tender exception of Rose, who died at thirty-six.

Possibly Rose's cancer was too advanced when it was discovered, but we preferred to believe that she postponed treatment so that she could spend a few more months with her babies. She was a heroine in the minds of many family women who came after her. France had its Joan of Arc; we had our Rose.

In the days of cheap and abundant manual labor, a greater division of roles existed between man and woman than today. Rosa Kelley and her sisters were left to tend their traditionally huge gardens and to perform traditional tasks while the men labored. Should a woman need her wash water heated and hauled, it was her husband, son or hired man that saw to the task. Should anything go amiss, a man was close at hand to handle the situation. Ladies remained in the house and yard, men, in the field. But farm life held enough work for everyone, man or woman.

The Borchard sisters enjoyed a close-knit sisterhood where one might drop in on another at any time with recipe, apron pattern or her delicious German coffee cake—thin slabs of sweet yeast dough covered with thick cream and sugar, sprinkled with cinnamon and baked to a golden custard. A pan could disappear in a trice when hungry boys passed through the kitchen and cut themselves a quarter-pan slice. The ladies visited each other and often stayed for a meal. Sometimes they stayed overnight and helped each other put up peaches when the fruit ripened, or sewed a wedding dress, or nursed a sick child through the night.

When their mother died, the Borchard sisters learned to depend upon themselves. They dispensed advice, worried about their hands and the effects of the burning rays of the sun on their complexions, looked out for each other's children and, when the time came, some made their wills with nephews and nieces in mind.

A woman's lot didn't improve with age, especially for childless women like Silas's sister, Elizabeth. Aunt Lizzy, as she was called, had been abandoned or divorced by a husband in Texas. For as long as she was able, she worked as a ranch cook for Ida and Caspar Borchard. As she got older, Aunt Lizzy suffered from nerves, possibly agoraphobia, and seldom left her house.

Her house was a one-room shack enclosing 144 square feet of living space, including a lean-to kitchen with a kerosene two-burner stove and a bit of board for a work counter. A wooden walk of loose, mismatched boards connected the house to an outhouse. The shack perched in a hollow off of Ventu Park Road, on the other side of a dry creekbed. In the winter, rains swelled the creek, isolating Lizzy from the town. It was a challenge for drivers to get their cars up to speed to cross the creek in order to bring her supplies.

Every year or two, Lizzy's sister, Minny, would arrive from Arizona with a small carpetbag containing her entire wardrobe, consisting of two fancy black-beaded dresses from the turn of the century. She still owned the same two taffeta dresses, or others similar that she picked up at thrift stores, when she died in the 1940s. Hopelessly outdated, covered with elaborate beading, they were museum pieces even at the time she wore them.

Lizzy and Minnie, along with anyone else living there and any visitor that happened by for the day to bring supplies and news, sat on the beds and did needlework or quilted while the visitor's children played in the dirt outside. One year the County paid Lizzy fifteen dollars a month to take in two teenage girls who needed a place to live.

Many valley residents claimed a relationship to Aunt Lizzy by marriage or by circumstance. Whoever was passing by brought kerosene and ice for her icebox, produce from their garden, staples from the market. When someone butchered, a portion of meat was set aside for her. Social Security was a concept that came too late for all the Aunt Lizzys of the era. No matter; people of the Conejo took care of their own.

Chapter Nine
Faith of Our Fathers

In the Conejo, fortune did not grace all its inhabitants with a steady hand. Only a few years before Silas drove his automobile into the Valley, his brother, John Reily Kelley, Jr. and sister-in-law Lucy made their way to California from Oklahoma in a covered wagon.

Known to everyone as Aunt Lucy, she had come to California in the 1890s from Texas and then returned home. In 1910 she made the trip again, in the same covered wagon pulled by a team of sturdy horses. Before they finally settled in the Conejo, the couple made the trip three times, searching for a way to make a living for their family of six. In the course of their travels the family increased to ten children.

In visits to the Borchard sisters, Aunt Lucy shared stories of her travels that became family legends. She recalled mounted Indians that watched them from top of mesas as their wagon rolled along at the pace set by their worn-out horses. She remembered that the horses were not good travelers because they lacked stamina and suffered from thirst more than mules, but they were cheaper to purchase. For better or worse, horses were the best they could afford.

On one trip, Aunt Lucy carried two barrels of yeast starter for making bread. When their water barrels ran dry, she fed her thirsty children the yeast starter, a slurry with enough water in it to sustain them until they reached the next water source. The memory of that yeast made it a comfort food for her. She craved it for the rest of her life.

After one crossing, the family arrived at Long Beach desperately poor and starving. One of the children managed to bring down a sea gull, the only food at hand, with a stone. Plucked, the bird's flesh was black and rubbery. They tried roasting it over a small fire that they built on the sand, but even cooked, the gull was so tough that they threw it to the dogs. The dogs, she remembered, would not eat it.

Years earlier on his trip west, Caspar Borchard's brother, Christian, was involved in an incident that haunted him throughout his lifetime. His dog killed an Indian that attacked his covered wagon. He spoke of it only once or twice and bitterly regretted the accident. He did not wish to be known for this one deed. When pressed to tell the story, he let it be inferred that his big black dog chased the marauding Indian away.

In 1938, Aunt Lucy was seventy years old. Although she died long before we were born, her spirit and her stories live in the memories of her great-nephews and great-nieces, and in those of us who can claim no relationship except by association. We feel privileged to have had a Great-great Aunt Lucy who makes our lives richer because she links us to the past. Our children will never know their great uncles or aunts. Their Aunt Lucys have vaporized in the social isolation of modern-day California.

The connection from my great-great grandfather to my generation is not a vague tale of the land. Our tradition is as close as a walk through our dining room. In 1960, two ancient gentlemen, Great-great uncles Caspar, Jr. and Frank Borchard stopped by our house near Paso Robles to share a noontime meal and to see the farm which we had moved to after we left the Conejo.

After lunch, Caspar lifted up the tablecloth to examine the long, battle-scarred table that he and his wife, Ida, had given my parents years earlier. Caspar pointed to a wedge in the wood about the size of a boy's penknife. My mother hated the flaw and always covered it up with a tablecloth when she had company.

Caspar and Frank laughed and recalled the day that they had been rough-housing and one of them knocked the piece out. Their mother had boxed their ears and sent them off without dinner. For as long as she owned the table, their mother, Theresa Maring Borchard, had covered the wedge. When her son, Caspar, Jr. and Ida needed a table for their growing family, she gave it to him because he had ruined it.

From that day on, my mother left the cloth off her table. The wedge, like the old men who told the story, became a proud part of her heritage. Perhaps I will inherit the table. Maybe it will go to my brother, Matt. Whoever gets it will recall a mother, in 1888, boxing a little boy's ears for knocking the wedge out. More than a century later we remain connected.

As my brother Matt grew into adolescence he bore a striking resemblance to Great-uncle John Kelley. My brother was a carrier of family genes that rendered him dark and tall, serious and slow talking, just like Nana's brother. When my brother's twin boys were born, also fraternal like Uncle John and Nana, we understood that the event was not a coincidence. Their genes are alive and well in my brother's line.

Like farmers who faithfully save seeds from a time before biotechnology interfered with natural selection, we record our oral histories and save them in hopes that someone will want to know their roots. It is surprising what people recall about long-ago events. Everyone seems to have a different version. Each version, I believe, carries a nugget of truth.

When children weren't present, Conejo ladies whispered about things that were never discussed openly, shameful events and oddities that occurred when the Valley was sparsely settled. They shared stories about nocturnal visitors who bailed out of bedroom windows when the man of the house drove up, the inbred family with oddish children, men and women no better than they had to be.

Several families had children prone to seizures. My mother has clear recollection of several children sent home from school after seizing, of church members who suffered seizures during service, of families with secrets that the community pretended not to know.

When curiosity ran high and facts were sketchy, the citizens of the Conejo conjectured, as they had done with the deaths of the Olsen children. My mother wonders if the seizures might have been the result of birth trauma or prolonged labor during home deliveries.

The ability of the community to mind its collective business seemed to allow people to live within its narrow confines. In an era where every move was noticed by someone, secrets were kept, allowances were made. People believed in a basic tenant of humankind, that people are neither all good nor all bad, but given instead to foibles that allow no one to cast the first stone.

Living close to her extended family made Nana close-mouthed, even in matters that she could have shared. After her death, we cousins tried to piece together the quilt of Nana's life, adding our recollections like swatches stitched together with laughter and amazement. It was strange, the parts of herself that she chose to share. Her life had remained constant for so many years. She died before the advent of rapid social change. I believe she didn't share details because she didn't think they would seem interesting.

A cousin recalls lunchtime at Nana's kitchen table, Nana flirting with Grandpa, teasing him about her other beaus and seeing a flare of jealousy in his reaction to something they hadn't discussed in fifty-five years together.

American farming is said to have reached its high point from the mid 1910s to the early 1920s. It was a good time to be raising crops, especially on land owned without burden of a mortgage. The struggle to make a living at farming involved testing new crops. Just like today, farmers experimented and dropped those that proved unprofitable. Like farmers everywhere, Conejo farmers were constantly changing their crop profile, especially after electricity allowed the Kelleys to drill a huge, communal well in the center of the family flat land.

From the 1930s through the war years, Nana tried various endeavors to earn money. She raised rabbits and chickens, she planted a large garden and sold the produce in town. Finally, she took in foster children whose fathers could pay for them to stay in a congenial country environment.

In 1927, Grandpa and his neighbors built a barn to store winter hay and to shelter his sheep in safety from coyotes at night. Eventually his flock increased to four hundred. Sheep seemed to be profitable and they required little care. Gradually, Grandpa fenced and cross-fenced the farm and retained only 40 acres for cultivation.

In the early 1940s he rented grazing rights in Chatsworth for his sheep and spent much of the summer camping with his four-year-old son, Neil, while they tended the flock. Sometimes Nana drove out on weekends and brought supplies.

Grandpa hired a sheepherder, a fellow from Kentucky who was diligent in his duties but who didn't own a pair of shoes. One day he ran after some sheep and became stranded in a patch of puncture vine or goat's-head. Grandpa had to haul the herder out of the field with a fireman's carry. He went to town and returned with a pair of used shoes. The Kentuckian spent a day nursing a fever induced by the poison that had entered his bloodstream.

Uncle Neil learned his trade at his father's side. Later, he worked a few summers for the Peterson Brothers in the Norwegian Colony, baling hay with their stationary baler. His favorite job was driving the two horses that pushed the buck rake supplying shackled hay to the stationery engine-run baler. It took six to eight men to run the baler. Labor was scarce. It was a time when even young boys could earn a day's wages.

Later, in high school, Neil sheared his neighbor's sheep, traveling from farm to farm to clip their small herds with his electric shears. In many ways, Neil reaped the benefits of his father's hard work, but he also inherited an industrious nature and his father's common sense.

Before the Norwegian Grade was built, the area from the Norwegian Colony northwest to Somis was badlands where highwaymen could rob travelers and disappear. My grandfather recalled being accosted by a bank robber who was escaping the sheriff in Los Angeles. As a small boy, Grandpa was walking to school when a man crossed his path, armed with a pistol with a long barrel. Shortly after he disappeared, a posse followed in close pursuit. They caught up with the robber down the road and took him prisoner. Grandpa continued his long walk home with a story to tell.

In 1902, when he was seven, Grandpa's parents determined that he should attend the Fremontville School in Moorpark. The distance was seven miles. They felt he was too young to be entrusted with a horse so he had no option except to walk—alone. There were no other children of school age to walk with. His sisters were sick and the Pederson boys weren't yet old enough for school.

Grandpa presented an enigma for the Moorpark School Board because he didn't speak English. The school board members didn't know his father and poor immigrant farmers had little influence on political decisions. Grandpa was allowed to enroll with a proviso. He would attend for a year to learn the language, then begin first grade the following year. His parents must provide transportation to school.

Small and withdrawn, Grandpa experienced anti-immigrant sentiments first-hand that shaped his attitudes toward the less fortunate for his entire life.

He was too shy to ask for a ride on the buggies that the local ranchers' sons drove to school. When he worked up his courage, they refused, even though they were going in the same direction. Some days he would wait until the buggy set off, then run and jump onto the axle and hope that he could hide. If they noticed, the boys scratched and beat at his hands until he was forced to drop off and make his long way home fighting tears.

The following year, his teacher moved to Simi and gave him a ride to the crossroads, cutting the walk by five miles.

At the Tierra Rejada, a wild portion of land at the base of what would later become the Norwegian Grade, a barbed wire fence divided two ranches. On one side, small brown bears lived in the brush. On the other side of the fence a farmer named Lapeyre ran longhorn cattle. Each day, morning and night, Grandpa had to decide which side of the fence he should walk on, the bear side or the long-horn side. One day he came over the ridge and found himself face-to-face with a bear. He forgot all about school, turned around and ran home.

Some days, Mrs. Lapeyre would invite him in to have something to eat and drink.

When the days grew shorter, his teacher dismissed him early from school early at 2:00 p.m. (instead of the usual 4:00 p.m.) so that he could get home before dark. On days that he played along the way, his mother walked part of the distance to see what kept him. It wasn't until he was grown that he realized she was worried. He thought she simply liked to walk with him.

With her daughters crippled and dying at home, perhaps his mother walked because Grandpa carried all of her hopes for her children's futures.

Grandpa attended Fremontville School for a couple of years, until he was considered old enough to be trusted with a horse. Then he rode to Timber School for two years with the Pederson boys, until their father died and they moved to Santa Barbara.

At Timber, he met a cute little girl with long braids and a lot of brothers who were always teasing her. On his first day, the boys were playing 'Annie Over', and they raced around the school building to catch the ball, knocking the little girl down. Grandpa leaned to pick Nana up, brush her off and continue the game without breaking stride. It was 1906. She was six years old and in first grade; he was eleven and in fourth grade.

In 1912, Grandpa was a teenager riding his horse up the Norwegian Grade when he came around a bend and noticed a wagon overturned in the roadway. A big, red-headed man lay on the ground, apparently unconscious. Above him stood a man with a rock in his hands, preparing to bash the skull of the fallen man. Grandpa was farm-boy strong and quick-thinking. He managed to disarm the man and secure him to the wagon.

When the redheaded man revived, he introduced himself as Robert Emmett Clark, the Sheriff of Ventura County. The would-be murderer was his prisoner. "Red Bob" Clark prided himself on not manacling his prisoners. In most cases, prisoners honored the trust, but this one was of another mind. Grandpa and Red Bob secured him and repaired the wagon, and the Sheriff went on his way.

Although the story never made the newspaper, Grandpa shared it with his grandsons on a few occasions. To them, his nonchalant heroism seemed like that of a war hero who didn't bother to collect his battle ribbon.

In later years, Bob Clark's grandson, William, served as State Supreme Court Justice, President Ronald Reagan's Chief of Staff, and as National Security Advisor. It seems ironic that the sight where Oscar Olsen undoubtedly saved Bob Clark's life is within a half-mile from the present sight of the Ronald Reagan Library.

Today, the view from the Ronald Reagan Library looks out on one side across miles of barren land, golden humpbacks in a waterless sea of grass. On the other side, endless miles of houses stretch to the Los Angeles city limits.

During the time of the Norwegian Colony, Moorpark Road ran from Thousand Oaks to Olsen Road. Later the County graded it, but travelers' wheels, rain and frost caused it to washboard so that the four-mile trip from Highway 101 seemed much farther. The road dissecting the Colony was named Olsen Road after my great-grandfather because he donated the right-of-way.

Grandpa's was the first area family to be serviced with natural gas. He allowed the gas lines to be trenched across his land on the condition that the gas company hook his house to the line. The line traversing his land was the main line into Los Angeles. Someone must have agreed because Grandpa's house was plugged directly onto the line with no offset.

Many years later, in the late 1970s, a construction crew remodeling Grandpa's house accidentally hit the connector and a gas plume spewed into the air with enough force to blow up the neighborhood. The contractor was afraid to start a car to go for help so someone ran across the fields to a neighbor's to use their phone. When the servicemen arrived, the main line had to be turned off in the grainfield. That was the first time anyone realized the potential danger.

Janss Road was nonexistent until the Janss Ranch was developed in the late 1950s. Some confusion existed about the spelling of their name. In newspaper articles and letters, the name appeared spelled "Janns" as often as "Janss". Sometimes reporters spelled it "Jans".

The Janss family owned much land and hired local men to cowboy their cattle, hoe their beanfields and farm their diverse holdings. Uncle Charlie worked for them until he retired. Their family house set up a long driveway, a sprawling ranch house just visible from Highway 101. Dagney and Peter Janss attended Timber School with little fanfare.

My cousin, Johnny Kelley, Jr., or Nonnie, as we called him, was Peter's friend. When they were in the fourth grade, Peter's father flew his two boys and Nonnie in the Janss airplane to Disneyland. The year was 1955; Disneyland had been open for about a month.

On Monday following the excursion, my brother and I pumped Nonnie for details. He seemed most impressed by the hotel. The three boys had jumped on the beds and had pillow fights until the down pillows split open and covered the room with fluff. Peter's father called room service and the maids moved them into another room for the night.

Urban development of the Conejo began slowly. Prior to 1922, a few large ranches and farms dotted the valley. They were divided or sold as the need arose, but large ranches dominated the landscape. These were the Janss Ranch with its horses and cattle; The Lang Ranch with its grain and cattle; the McCrea Ranch, cattle and grain; the Peterson Ranch, chickens, citrus and grain; the Hunt Ranch; the Borchard Ranches; the Freidrich Ranch. The area was a pure agrarian society with attendant drawbacks and benefits.

Some of the ranches were still owned by the original owners. Others had changed hands in the Depression years, when banks overextended credit and called in their notes, and the ranchers were unable to repay their loans.

Even into 1950, Thousand Oaks consisted of little more than three bars, a market, the Redwood Lodge, the Lion Farm, a gas station, Reverend Elver's Community Church and an elementary school. The children bought penny candy from an old man named Nickle Brown, who sold ice cream and candy through a little pass-through window in the front of his house.

Henry Crowley inherited land in the Thousand Oaks area from his father in 1906. He purchased his brother's and sister's portions of the inheritance. It was his son, Frank, born in Newbury Park, who sold two large blocks of the farm in 1922 for a housing development. One was developed as Greenwich Village in Thousand Oaks and the other later sold to a development team named Culver and Sturges.

At the time, Great-uncle John had leased the land and had planted it to barley. The land was offered for sale to lot-hungry Los Angelenos with the proviso that the owners could not take possession until the crop was harvested.

A frenzy of land fever ensued. Culver and Sturges paid for busses or touring cars to run from Los Angeles. The developer's wives served lunch in their houses to the prospective buyers, and the excitement attracted both lookers and buyers.

The buyers ignored the condition of sale and trudged into the ripening grain-fields to mark their lots. The new buyers came on Sundays and planted grapevines and rose bushes in the midst of the barley. Uncle John and his bride, Babe, could do little more than watch.

Finally it was time for John to harvest his crop. Although he exercised such care as he felt the situation required, nearly all of the vines and roses were destroyed when the crop was cut. He seemed unable to control his horses and they overpowered him, taking the rows right down the middle of the vines. In later years, whenever he told the story his eyes twinkled with regret over the ruination of the bushes.

Eventually, he purchased a house from E.B. Parks on Oak View Drive, in the heart of "Old Town" (Thousand Oaks). He and Babe lived there until they built a home on his land on Borchard Road, next to his sisters and mother.

Chapter Ten
A Thousand Oaks

From its inception, the subdivision of Thousand Oaks attracted a strange assortment of investors. Many farmers viewed their new neighbors as misfits with dubious pasts and secrets to hide. Lou Long, for instance, lived in an old ambulance. Others were circus people drawn by the employment opportunities of the Lion Farm. For the first few years, the Valley buzzed with rumors about its more colorful citizens, those who fled bad debts and investments gone awry with someone else's money, or the law.

As the town began to grow, it needed a name. Developers offered a prize of five dollars and a small lot for the best name. The winner was a young boy who attended the Conejo School, named Bobby Harrington. It was to be called Thousand Oaks.

A few years later, Fred Kelley, Jr. and some of his teenage buddies decided to count the trees. They started in the center of town and worked outward until they had satisfied their curiosity. Fred has forgotten the actual count, but they found at least a thousand, more than enough to justify the town's name. Some old timers contend that, at the time there were probably twenty thousand oaks dotting the Conejo Valley.

Before Thousand Oaks existed, the El Grande Hotel provided a stopover for travelers that dated back to 1876. Constructed with redwood, the Hotel's wood was shipped from northern California lumber mills to Hueneme, then freighted over the Conejo Grade in large wagons and teams of draft horses.

Thousand Oaks was conceived in a burst of rugged individualism. For the first years, people lived in makeshift tents while they constructed their houses with limited resources. Residents had to brave the winding Conejo Grade or the Norwegian Grade to go to Camarillo for their groceries and staples.

The farmers in the valley ignored the commotion as best they could. The development going on around them did not increase the value of their land to them. They had no use for the Lion Farm or their new neighbors. They stayed home and farmed.

Newbury Park was older and more established than its upstart neighbor to the southeast. A few houses and stores existed, wedged between the Borchard lands on the south and the Freidrich land on the north. The settlement wasn't really a town.

Behind Newbury Park's main street, Ventu Park was a budding real estate development. The five-hundred-acre development was divided into four thousand lots, some so small they were unbuildable. On the map, the lots lined out in tidy squares that ignored the hilly terrain and deep, eroded crevices and brush. The forty-foot square lots were only large enough to build a tiny cabin. Lots sold to movie stars who wanted a rustic retreat, adventurous types who could do without the trappings of luxury and people who needed a cheap place to build.

During the 1940s, one of the male members of the New York Rothschilds built a big house in Ventu Park and lived in relative seclusion while the town speculated about his reasons for rusticating in the area. The idea circulated that he might be an illegitimate son or a homosexual. His lack of employment suggested that his family fortune supported his lifestyle. Carrol Pruett, CEO of Midstate Bank recalled to my Uncle Neil that he hoed weeds for Mr. Rothschild as a boy.

Ventu Park served as low-income housing during the Depression and War years. Eventually, lots were combined to allow larger houses. With suitable permanent housing, the Conejo Valley began to grow.

Newbury Park was never incorporated as a city, but was left to the mercy of County officials, who seemed to take little interest. While the rest of the county developed, Newbury Park remained little more than a wide spot in the road. During the 1950s, rumors persisted that County officials refused to allow Newbury Park to expand because of a feud with would-be developers. The town of Newbury Park lay entangled in legal limbo while the rest of the Conejo exploded with planned developments.

Citizens of the Conejo Valley traveled to Oxnard when they needed to be married, buried, attend high school or obtain supplies. The baptismal certificates of Nana and her brothers indicate that babies were taken to Oxnard for christening. In the late 1920s, the Camarillo family built St. Mary Magdelan Catholic Church in Camarillo. Marriages took place in Camarillo or Oxnard, burials in the Santa Clara Cemetery in Oxnard, the nearest Catholic cemetery. Protestants held services in Thousand Oaks. Lutherans buried their dead in Ivy Lawn Cemetery in Montalvo.

Thousand Oaks was without a high school until the 1950s. Until then, students made a choice between attending school in Oxnard or Moorpark. A Mr. Smith, whom everyone called "Smitty", parked the bus next to his house in Thousand Oaks and drove the route to Moorpark. Some years the route was 50 miles one way. Smitty began his route in Thousand Oaks, drove along Moorpark Road to Santa Rosa Valley and into Moorpark. It was a long ride that began for some students before sun-up. Another bus went through Camarillo, Camarillo Heights, Bolcan Canyon and to Moorpark. Following construction of Camarillo High School, this route was discontinued.

In the early days, recreation was home-grown wherever people could find it. On the Hunt Ranch, a steep canyon, *a salto,* (Spanish for "jumping off place"), featured a creek with a waterhole. The *Salto* reigned as the summer meeting place for young and old alike. Locals accessed it by a road through the Janss Ranch or by way of the Hunt Ranch Road. Men fished for trout, women brought picnic lunches and cooled watermelon in the running water. Children spent hot summer afternoons jumping off rope swings into the swimming hole.

One mother noted in her journal how the swimming hole and the ranch creeks made life easier for her. At the time, the water table was higher and even some of the smaller creeks ran year around.

For those who could afford it, refinements came later. Seminole Hot Springs, near Agoura, was developed as a spa. Its sulfur water spewed from the earth into natural hot tubs to soothe sore muscles and arthritic joints. Wealthy Jewish urbanites and movie people from Los Angeles flocked to the Hot Springs on weekends to see and be seen.

Those who could not afford to buy their own rented the spa's black wool swimsuits. Nana, and later, my mother, recalled the ugly, scratchy swimming suits and soaking in the sulfuric, rotten-egg-smelling waters.

Eventually, Public Health laws required changes that the Hot Springs deemed unreasonable and the bathhouse went the way of progress.

Long after the disappearance of the highwaymen who had threatened Rosa Kelley on her trek back to the Conejo in 1901, Agoura and Calabasas remained a long stretch of badland. In the early days, there was only the Nine-Mile Café and the Triunfo Store. Later, at Brents Junction, Wonies Café served as an oasis on the journey between the Conejo and Hollywood. Trips to Los Angeles were not taken lightly until the advent of the automobile.

The Calabasas was hot and arid before the Colorado River and Owens Valley water turned Northern Los Angeles County into a land of hybrid trees and patented roses. The 1800s farmers had good reason to eschew the area in favor of the fertile farm lands to the northwest.

Calabasas was cattle country or sheep country, depending on the landowner's preference. Mr. Poyer ran sheep on his ranch. One of his hired hands was an old cowboy named Doc Dinsmore, whose wife taught school near Moorpark. Even today, in towns with paper-pretty names like Mission Viejo, broken adobe circles mark the abandoned ruins of holding pens where sheep once grazed.

The Russell Ranch (which never saw a sheep run on its thousands of acres) was sold to the Hearsts and eventually developed as Westlake Village. Depending on whose opinion one seeks, the Westlake development marked the salvation or the death knell for the Conejo farmer.

In its early years, Skinner and Belle Hollaway ran a dairy farm with the help of a milker known as Big Pockets. Every morning, milkers woke at 3:00 a.m. and herded the cows to a milking shed. Afterwards, they drove the cows, with empty udders and bellies, into downtown Thousand Oaks. There they spent the day grazing along the streets of Thousand Oaks, crossing between cars and between buildings in Old Town. At five o'clock in the evening, Big Pockets herded the cows back for milking and penned them for the night. The system worked well. People braked for the cattle and the byways were kept clipped. Pedestrians watched for steaming cowpies.

Eventually refrigeration and pasteurization laws became stricter. Skinner died, and traffic in the town increased. Bell Hollaway sold her cows to Chase Dairy in Oxnard and began a profitable business hauling horses. It is unknown what became of Big Pockets.

As a girl, I remember seeing Belle, a short, plump woman, dressed in men's Levis with wide, turned-up cuffs and worn out cowboy boots. Practicality ruled in every line of her body. She smoked, she drank, she swore. She went by the name of "Ma". A big-hearted woman of the West, she saw to it that people got what they needed. Long before she served as honorary mayor, she kept down-and-outers employed, headed up community-spirited events and added her brand of hospitality to Thousand Oaks.

During the 1920s, a Negro man, Mr. Henderson, opened the Greentree Inn

next to where the Redwood Lodge was later built on Ventura Boulevard. A digni-
fied man, Mr. Henderson had been butler to a wealthy man named Mr. Pealer.

When the old man died, his daughter, Miss Pealer, and Henderson came to
the Conejo and started the Greentree Inn with her money. Mr. Henderson was
an excellent innkeeper and chef, widely traveled, and quite sophisticated for the
budding town. Miss Pealer added her artistic talents to creating ambiance in the
popular Inn.

For a few years during the Great Depression, Grandpa Olsen worked at the
Greentree Inn, in the evenings when he finished his chores, or between farming
seasons. He waited tables, washed dishes, and worked large parties and banquets.
Grandpa's motives seemed to concern some of his neighbors. He needed the
money, but more than that, Mr. Henderson was having difficulty hiring help.
Grandpa endured some taunting and mild threats by citizens who thought he
should stick to farming and stop associating with Negroes.

By 1929, a number of Ku Klux Klansmen had moved into Thousand Oaks.
Suddenly Henderson became the target of a vocal minority who objected to a
black businessman. They also noticed his white employee.

My mother still recalls the day that two businessmen threatened to beat up
Grandpa and his family if he "didn't stop working for a nigger." Stubborn, too
proud to stand in the Depression lines like many others, Grandpa refused to quit.
The family grew wary of strangers coming to the farm. They did most of their
trading in Moorpark and avoided Thousand Oaks except when Grandpa worked
a shift.

By the end of 1929, the Greentree Inn was closed down, but money was
apparently not an issue. The KKK circulated a rumor that Mr. Henderson and
Miss Pealer's relationship was more than a business arrangement. In a flurry of
anti-black sentiment, Henderson was driven out of the Inn. The payments for the
land had been made on time, but Henderson leased the land from a local land
company. The owners succumbed to public pressure and cancelled his lease.

With no place to live, Henderson and Miss Pealer found their way to
Grandpa's ranch. They retrieved as many personal possessions as they could
manage and set up housekeeping on a plot of land behind the Olsen's apricot
orchard with another woman, a Miss Nielson.

Within a few days they had built a house out of three one-room bungalows
that they salvaged from their Greentree Auto Court, a row of rental units behind
the Inn. Grandpa helped slide the bungalows onto skids and used his automobile

to drag them from Thousand Oaks along Moorpark Road.

Henderson and Grandpa nailed the bungalows together to form a single house. Miss Pealer draped the walls with genuine Navajo Indian blankets for insulation. An artist, she and her friend filled the rooms with artistic sculptures of her own creation. Miss Pealer sometimes served tea, and showed my mother treasures from her travels.

In time, the citizens of Thousand Oaks moved on to other interests. Henderson got a job at Lake Sherwood, and he and Miss Pealer built a lovely home on the west side of the highway, far up on a hillside near the Russell Ranch.

Throughout the history of the Conejo, coincidence twists and twines like ribbon, linking past to present, one person to another. Memories were long, but so were friendships. In the late 1940s, my Aunt Arthelia took a job at American Commercial & Savings Bank in Moorpark, working for a branch manager named Aloyisis Honerkamp.

In 1950, a young Mexican man, Mike Loza, came to see Mr. Honerkamp about borrowing five hundred dollars. It was his dream to start a Mexican restaurant. He felt he could make a go of it, but he had applied with several banks and had been turned down. Mr. Honerkamp sized up the man and gave him the loan.

A few years passed. Arthelia married the banker's son (my uncle, Alloys 'Jack' Honerkamp). Senor Loza outgrew his little restaurant in Moorpark, called, simply, Mike Loza's, and built a larger one in Camarillo. It became a landmark, El Tecolote. For years afterwards, Senor Loza would not accept a dime for dinner whenever the Honerkamps stopped to eat on their way home to Whittier.

Eventually, the elder Mr. Honerkamp retired from American Commercial & Savings and began a second career with Bank of America. For several years he visited Timber and Conejo schools every Thursday for "Bank Day". He provided each student with a savings passbook and a sturdy cardboard savings envelope with a red string fastener wound around two cardboard buttons. It all seemed very official. Because he was my cousins' grandfather, I was privileged to be able to call this distinguished man, "Grandpa Ollie" as they did.

On Wednesdays, our teacher reminded us to bring our envelopes with at least twenty-five cents inside. The next day Grandpa Ollie carried our deposits to the Bank of America in Camarillo. On his way home from work he dropped the empty envelopes at the school office with our deposit noted in our savings passbook.

Making a regular deposit became a point of honor in my family. No matter how poor we were, we found four quarters, one for each of my sisters and brother. I overheard my mother and my Aunt Arthelia talking. The bank had put Grampa Ollie on notice; he would lose his job if Bank Day deposits didn't pick up. I added the money I earned picking blackberries at my parent's roadside stand and managed to save $132.26 by the time I left the Conejo in 1959.

Chapter Eleven
Nostalgia

In an era without unemployment insurance, when full employment meant survival, people of earlier generations worked for as long as they were able. Widows cooked for harvest crews to support their children. Old men who ended up land-wealthy boasted of their early days hopping bottles for dairies, poisoning gophers and squirrels for ranches, hoeing beans on dryland ranches, picking and pitting apricots, doing a variety of temporary and long-term jobs that provided a living. Resumes were unheard of in those days; a friendly word was all that was needed. People depended on each other to help out, bumper crops or bust.

Later, the movie industry brought money into the valley at a time when farm prices fell below the expense of production. During those years, land values were low, but so were taxes. People needed less to be happy. Farmers kept an eye out for a chance to buy more land, but few were selling. Mostly, they sat on their acreage and tried to make a living.

Our family farmland in the Conejo was as cheap as anywhere else. We had no choice but to farm. Ours was not a family that aspired to go into commerce.

Some people tried making a fast buck, but word spread quickly in a farming community. For a brief period in the mid-1930s, four Jewish men ran a grocery store with exceptional prices. Great-uncle Fred and his family counted themselves as savvy customers. One day, in 1938, the men's photographs appeared on the front page of the Times. They had been arrested in Oxnard, in possession of four trucks filled with stolen groceries from Safeway, A&P Market, and two other grocery stores. With some embarrassment, Great-uncle Fred moved his trade back to the other grocery store.

The Conejo gained a reputation as a colony for movie stars. Natives and the famous existed side-by-side. Joel McCrea was my grandfather's neighbor. His ranch headquarters sat behind whitewashed outbuildings at the base of the Norwegian Grade. We never called him "Joel". Neither was he "Mr. McCrea". Everyone called him, "Joel McCrea".

Joel McCrea was a regular neighbor. He sent his children to school along with other farmers' children, but he augmented their education by paying for class trips to Los Angeles museums. He paid for his sons' classmates to enjoy their first ice cream sodas and banana splits. Whenever his latest movie came out, he arranged for classes to take a field trip to the Moorpark movie house to see a special showing.

Across Grandpa's fence on the neighboring Janss Ranch, a movie town was built as a western movie set. It was a make-believe town with buildings with false fronts. Tarps covered the back wall of each room to keep out the rain and to allow cameras and crews access.

From Nana's front porch we could watch stagehands roll paper *maché* boulders from a horse-drawn hay wagon. Within minutes the workers converted bare hillsides into rocky bluff and canyons. When the cameras rolled, we watched riders ride pell-mell down the "canyon", pursued by a band of Indians who had been idling beside their horses five minutes earlier.

The dynamics of the set were easy to define. The cowboys wore white hats, the bad men wore black. The movie Indians were invariably the bad guys, with bloodcurdling yelps and flying rubber arrows. Movie Indians wore lots of feathers and war paint and looked suspiciously like Caucasians with bad wigs.

Filming lasted only a minute or two. Across the fence we could watch the action, but the director's orders were lost in the wind.

Television was brand new. Nothing was real, nothing was permanent. The plots and action, the fake backdrops and sound effects were so amateurish that, in later years, our children laughed at our naiveté. But it fooled us. If filmmaking was an illusion, we were happy to be beguiled.

In the early movies, the plot was the thing. The camera captured long views of chases with a generous dose of raw action and scenery. Eventually, sophisticated audiences demanded tighter, character-driven treatment and filmmaking returned to studios and sound stages. Far sooner than we were ready to let them go, film crews picked up their movie sets and left the Conejo.

For twenty years we watched the background of every TV western to see if we recognized the location.

One morning in 1957, neighborhood dogs alerted us before our ears caught an improbable blend of syncopated drumming and shouting. As my sisters and I watched at a bend in the road, a caravan of camels and elephants paraded past our house. For a week the air reverberated with strange bellowings in the canyon behind Borchard Road. Cecil De Mille was making a biblical movie with a cast of hundreds.

In my mother's childhood, as in most years before World War II, a circus train off-loaded at the depot in Moorpark and marched its elephants single file across Moorpark Road to the Lion Farm. Because they traveled by night, a man holding a lantern rode on the front elephant while another man, similarly equipped, rode the last elephant. The caravan snaked across the darkness with two tiny beacons bobbing a warning light for automobiles.

Nothing seemed too preposterous in those days. In the absence of laws specifically forbidding it, anything seemed allowable. If a caravan of elephants happened to be passing, the prudent motorist simply pulled over and waited.

In 1938, a movie scout stopped by Grandpa's farm and asked about staging a movie, *Wuthering Heights*, on the rugged bluffs overlooking his pasture. The scout wanted to rent the scenery and a few of the sheep that he saw grazing in Grandpa's pasture. Grandpa agreed, as did his two neighbors. The Samuel Goldwyn, Inc., Ltd., legal department drew up a contract for rental of the farmland, entrance rights, sheep and straw.

In early spring, a crew arrived to plant the hills with pots of heather. Overnight, the farm became the Scottish Highlands. Prop men laid false fences across the flats. They sprinkled fake snow on the cliffs, down-camera from the heather. A hundred yards of crag became an entire movie set.

On days that the eighty-five sheep appeared before the camera, my mother earned five dollars to herd them. For three days she was allowed to miss school. For her, that was the best part, even better than taking her meals in the catering line alongside stars whose faces she didn't recognize: Merle Oberon, Laurence Olivier and David Niven. At the time she had never attended a movie show.

Grandpa earned two hundred dollars for the use of his pastures. The sheep earned $2.50 each. Presumably he and Nana kept the money on their behalf. When *Wuthering Heights* was released, Grandpa was not sufficiently impressed to take his family to see it at the theater in Moorpark.

Other movies were made in the Norwegian Colony, including *How Green Was My Valley*, *Spartacus*, and several of the *Lassie* movie series, including another that my mother worked in, *Lassie Come Home.*

Life in the 1950s was idyllic for a kid growing up in the middle of her relatives. Opportunities were created by word of mouth. Someone mentioned to my father that the Lion Farm needed oat hay; from then on we made steady sales. On summer afternoons we delivered it down a narrow alley in Thousand Oaks, dodging elephant trunks flailing around the bed of the truck, grabbing for loose hay.

The locals didn't flock to Jungleland like the city crowds that came on Sundays. I attended only once, with my cousin, Jill Ashby. Her brother, Juney, drove us from Newbury Park in his new Isetta, gave us a twenty-dollar bill, and admonished us to bring back the change. We worked all day spending that twenty dollars. The entrance fee was $1.25. Sodas were a quarter—outrageous when compared to a dime a bottle at the grocery.

We ate until we were miserable, bought souvenirs, even gave the glamorous elephant trainer's assistant a dollar tip. We were fascinated by the way she allowed the elephant to wrap her scantily clad body in its trunk, twirling and dipping her as she maintained a confident smile. Eleven and ten years old at the time, Jill and I gazed at her and saw womanhood in all its glory: heavy mascara, short, pink leotard that revealed her considerable feminine charms, fishnet stockings and gold ballet shoes. Our dollar was less of a tip than homage paid to glamour and, although we couldn't identify it at the time, to sex appeal.

We still had four dollars and change left when Juney picked us up. He yelled at us all the way home. It was the best—and the worst—day of my life. Undoubtedly, Silas would have approved of his granddaughter and great-granddaughter enjoying themselves on such a grand scale. Great-great grandpa Borchard would have been horrified.

The hills that provided such good forage, and briefly bloomed with Samual Goldwyn's heather, were home to rattlesnakes that had been multiplying since Indian times. When Grandpa and his neighbors bladed ground to build his barn, eighteen rattlers slithered from a hole that the tractor opened in the bank. The snake dens were so dense that Grandpa had to use dynamite, the farmer's universal remedy for troublesome snakes and tree trunks. Rattlesnakes were a farmer's nemesis, notorious for striking the faces and legs of sheep and horses.

Before the era of environmental concerns, making a living took precedence over the vagaries of nature. Grandpa subscribed to the Audubon Society magazine, but he protected his crops and livestock with a vengeance.

When he was ten, Uncle Neil used his new BB gun to shoot blackbirds out of trees. He thought he would impress his classmates by telling them of his successful shots, ignoring the fact that he was president of the Audubon Club that year. He didn't make a distinction between the two deeds until his teacher pointed out his hypocrisy. His classmates were so upset with his shooting the birds that they impeached him.

An ancient Indian cave overlooked the farm from a bluff on the north edge of Grandpa's land. Painted with petroglyphs, the cave had held its secrets through the ages. Unbroken stone bowls and grinding stones lay buried in an area strewn with arrowheads and beads. We were allowed to visit the caves but not to touch. Grandpa taught us reverence for customs and cultures that we didn't understand. In later years, the caves were desecrated, but for the years that he owned the property, the caves remained a sacred spot.

To stand on the bluffs in the evening, when the setting sun reached its last fingers across the golden grass, was a proud and timeless moment. The winds churned the grass in the narrows and sang in the hills in a manner that made the cliffs seem alive. A century and a quarter after Nils Olsen embraced the land, native grasses still develop seedpods that drop to the earth before the next year's rains. Too steep for a tractor, the hills have held their identity throughout the ages.

The remoteness of the farm was a problem for my mother and her sister, Arthelia, two little girls growing up alone. During their childhood they were not the best of friends. Camaraderie came later, when they shared motherhood. During the early years, one was interested in the outdoors; the other remained content to stay indoors and learn domestic skills. One was Grandpa's helper, the other, Nana's. The division was clear and long-lasting.

During the Depression, farm families offered a safe haven for city families where both parents worked long hours to make a living. Los Angeles provided cash paychecks to the men who labored in the city, while farmers were cash poor. It was not unusual for the two factions to team up. Complete strangers boarded their children on farms and visited on weekends when they could afford the gasoline.

For several summers, Nana's cousin, Irene, sent her children, Nelda and Betty to the farm. Irene's father was one of Silas Kelley's brothers. Irene's husband worked as a foreman at a lemon packing shed near Pasadena.

When my mother spoke of her childhood years, Nelda and Betty figured so prominently into her memories that we felt we knew them. She took us to Los Angeles to visit Nelda when I was ten. I made shy advances towards her children while our mothers hoped we would become friends like they had been. We stood apace while shyness overwhelmed our attempts to talk.

Later, two brothers, Frank and Howard, fostered at Nana's house while their mother, Mazzie, operated a boat business out of Newport Beach. Their father was divorced from their mother and worked as a scientist at the Griffith Park Observatory. Aged five and seven—the same age as my Uncle Neil—they stayed for two years until their father remarried.

A few years later another boy, Timmy, came to stay for a year while his father worked in the Hollywood film industry.

Through similar circumstances, we began a life-long association with another family and gained an almost-aunt and three almost-cousins in the bargain. My aunt Arthelia's third grade best friend, Melva, lived with her grandparents on a ranch at the bottom of the Norwegian Grade. During the Depression, they lost the ranch and Joel McCrea bought it from the bank.

Through their children, Nana and Melva's mother, Boe, became friends. Boe was Protestant, artistic, divorced, fashion-conscious and chic. Nana was Catholic, grounded and practical. They seemed to have nothing in common; one had roots, the other had wings.

Boe met and married Frank Parker, a dashing, intelligent man who drove a sporty car, read voraciously, dressed in jodhpurs and boots to his knees and smoked marijuana. He moved his new family to Eagle Rock.

Through the years Boe and Melva returned to visit, sometimes coming to spend several weeks at the farm when Frank was out of work and disgusted with the bread lines in the city. When Frank was employed, Boe's home life sparkled with exotic ambiance that Nana's did not. Melva acquired a spider monkey, a turtle, pheasants and a goat, most of which eventually ended up on the Olsen Farm when she got tired of them.

Aunt Mary recalls spending two weeks with Boe in a remote writer's cabin in a canyon near Santa Monica while Boe wrote children's stories and sent them off to national magazines for publication. Boe drove her car into the mountains and loaded their provisions onto her burro. The process took several hours. By the time they set off along a narrow path beside a creek, it was nighttime. In total darkness, the burro picked its way to the cabin's front door. During the entire two weeks, Mary remembers seeing no visitors.

When Boe and Frank separated, Melva and her mother lived for three years in a small rental on Grandpa's property. Melva attended high school in Moorpark while Boe sold Raleigh products from her old Austin automobile. Later, she and Frank reconciled and moved to the Rock House in Thousand Oaks. He was later killed when a train struck his car.

Boe sewed with more ambition than skill. She had mastered only the basic rudiments of sewing but she created her wardrobe with a designer's flair. Most of her clothing came from Los Angeles thrift stores as old coats and dresses that she tore apart for the fabric. A black and white polka dot skirt became an elegant scarf right off the pages of *Vogue Magazine*.

In her later years she lost an eye to brain cancer and wore a neat white eye bandage beneath her eyeglasses. She wound her hair into an exquisite coil of snowy white, held neat-as-a-pin with combs and long hairpins. To me, she was glamour personified.

Nana, stuck at the edge of a valley, against hills that allowed her no view except her little Norwegian Colony, opened her house and her larder to this city friend. What she received must have been a fair trade because she and Boe struck a friendship that has flourished across four generations. Melva grew up, married, and began her own family. Her children seemed to arrive in years when my aunt didn't have a newborn, so they traded baby clothes back and forth. At every holiday and family celebration, clothing got sorted and passed on to the next wearer.

Melva married Frederick, who became an executive at RCA Records. He was the first man we ever knew who wore a suit to work. He was also a practicing Christian Scientist. For us Catholics, it was the most daring religion we'd encountered since Aimee Semple McPhearson began preaching in a revival tent on Charles Street in Moorpark in the late 1920s.

Frederick worked at the RCA building in Hollywood. Whenever my mother drove us past, my sisters and I would stare at the windows, expecting, I think, to see his name on the building. We were unsure about his position. I assumed that he was in charge of choosing the next big recording star. After all, hadn't he shaken hands with Elvis in 1959? Hadn't his father been a concert pianist who spent years-teaching voice and elocution to the silent screen stars when "talkies" came in? The merciless Depression evaporated the market for his father's skills as suddenly as the boom years had created it. But Frederick thrived in the post-World War II music technology and held an important job in the heart of Hollywood.

Frederick provided us children with the same sophistication that Frank Parker had for my mother's generation. He also supplied enormous boxes of Roman candles and fireworks that he picked up during trips to his trailer house in Rosarita Beach. He would shoot them off every Fourth of July when the night skies were ready for the show.

Certain events occurred each year that created a comforting cadence of tradition.

Easter was the big one, the event we called "Oscar's Picnic". It was always held at Nana's house, always outdoors, sometimes under the patio cover after we thrashed the flowerbeds for rattlesnakes and covered the tables with checkered tablecloths. Sometimes we picnicked on the *Wuthering Heights* bluffs where we could see the entire Norwegian Colony.

The celebration included Great-uncle Nick Olsen and his family from down the road and a host of familiar strangers whose relationship I never quite understood. Most were Nana's cousins of some sort. Sometimes we packed elaborate picnics with dishes laid out on tablecloths in the matted spring grass of the sheep pasture.

Fathers and children flew kites on the bluffs while mothers chatted and laid out the picnic. If the spring grass had grown tall enough, we took turns sliding down the slick grassy slopes on sheets of flat tin, rolled at the edges for safety. We ran up and down the earthen steps that the *Wuthering Heights* crew had dug to tote their equipment up the hill, twenty years earlier.

Later, we hunted Easter eggs in the pastures or on the lawns and picked oranges and lemons to take home. Before the party broke up, someone invariably brought out a Brownie camera and took a group photo with black and white film. We were the luckiest family alive.

I don't recall any of the Pederson's ever attending an Olsen family function. It seemed as though there was some sort of rift between the families by the time we grandchildren came along. Whatever it was, nobody spoke of it, probably a result of stubborn farmers who saw things differently.

Summers were spent at a beach cabin at Hollywood-by-the-Sea, near Oxnard. The development began with high aspirations that included laid-out streets, city water and cement sidewalks, until the Depression and World War II quelled investors' plans.

Nana spent two hundred fifty dollars of her inheritance on a 20'x70' lot in the 1940s. The lot had been one of the first sold and its location was ideal. The Pacific Ocean lay across the street, a quick walk over burning sand where waves broke in slow rolls and shimmered to a halt at the shore. The sand was white and crystalline, fine, as deep as children with shovels and buckets could dig, as smooth as a tropical beach.

In the years shortly after the War, Grandpa pitched a huge army surplus tent that covered half the lot. For years, summer and winter, the tent stood as a permanent fixture. When my mother was a girl, Nana placed dressers inside and stored swimsuits and clothing in the drawers. The tent stored cooking gear, pots and pans, lanterns and chairs.

Grandpa set a cast-iron cookstove in the sand and all meals were cooked outside. On each visit, he dug a hole down to water level, where the sand was damp and cool. In this hollow he placed a wooden box that served as a food cooler.

Great-uncle John and Aunt Babe Kelley parked their travel trailer on the lot and some of the children were allowed to sleep in it. No interloper ever bothered the site.

In the late 1940s, the tent began to rot. Grandpa constructed a one-room cabin with ship-lap siding and a tiny bathroom with a sheet metal shower stall. When his grandchildren began walking, he built a six-foot redwood fence to keep them contained, at the expense of his ocean view.

Hollywood-by-the-Sea was our front door to the Pacific Ocean. We saw wonder in every sight, smell and sound.

Two blocks down the street, a stone's throw beyond the chain link fence that served as base security, the U.S. Navy had dredged a channel from the deep-water port of Hueneme. Once each summer a low, bellowing horn signaled the departure of the U.S.S. Norton Sound, a battleship on its way to sea duty. We would race down the sidewalk and cluster against the fence to wave at the sailors standing at attention on the deck.

Once, my father stood beside me as we watched the Norton Sound sail. He snapped to attention and saluted the sailors, then recalled himself and glanced, half embarrassed, at me. Tears glistened in his eyes. My heart swelled with enormous pride, a child's pride. My father had sailed on such a ship before my birth.

The moment ended and we turned back toward the beach cabin as the ship's horn sounded long into the distance.

The next year, when the battleship passed, I imagined my father in his Navy whites, standing on deck while the wind whipped his kerchief.

My cousins and I visited the beach cabin as often as our mothers would take us. It was not a day-trip from the Conejo to Hollywood-by-the-Sea. If we went, we stayed at least the weekend. Our routine rarely varied. We would arrive, unlock the musty cabin and air it while we unpacked.

Nana shared the double bed there with my mother or my aunt, depending on who was pregnant at the time. Grandpa slept outside with the men and children, under canvas tarps fastened to the fence. If night fog dampened the bedding, he pitched a tent.

By the late 50s, the tent had to be disassembled at the end of each visit to protect against theft and vandalism.

By right of firstborn females, my cousin, Helen, and I were assigned a fold-down sofa bed that doubled as a booth for the dining table. This honor was not lost on us, but as the years went by, I longed for a chance to sleep outside on the sand in a sleeping bag, with the rest of the children. I did so on one or two occasions when one of the younger children was sick or sunburned, but Nana assigned the sleeping arrangements, and her rule was firm. If the sofa bed was negotiable, she and the mothers would spend their vacation adjudicating claims. Until we grew too tall to fit, my cousin and I shared the sofa.

Each morning our mothers smeared our exposed skin with baby oil and sent us out to play. When our cheeks burned, we remembered to wear our hats. When any one of us became cranky, we all had to take naps under a cluster of huge beach umbrellas that shaded a twenty-foot square section of the beach. Coppertone sun lotion was new on the market, but at $1.29 it was too expensive to dab more than a drop on burned shoulders. By the end of the week our fair Norwegian skins were peeling.

The vacation ended when the mothers' nerves were frayed beyond redemption by a half-dozen kids under the age of seven, cranky from lack of sleep and over-stimulation. What a wonderful vacation!

The first weekend in September marked the end of summer. Every year we celebrated with a huge family barbecue, a birthday cake, and hand-churned vanilla ice cream. Besides being my birthday, it was Labor Day weekend and the opening day of dove season.

Our family of farmers and hunters, city men, and adopted cousins took to the fields while the women made plans for Thanksgiving and Christmas.

The year I turned fourteen, I watched the men shoulder their shotguns and set off to hunt doves before dinner. The truth dawned on me in such a sudden, wrenching epiphany that my stomach plummeted in embarrassment. For all the years, it had been the opening day of dove season that attracted so many people. My birthday was coincidental.

Holidays brought the aunts and cousins back to the Conejo. Christmas didn't just happen. It was coordinated in long phone conversations and letters between Nana, my mother and the aunts.

By Christmas vacation, cousins began to arrive. By tradition, we waited until we were all together before rolling the sugar cookies. Nana had the dough ready when we arrived. With palpable anticipation we watched as she opened her refrigerator and pulled out mixing bowls of chilled, almond-flavored sugar cookie and gingerbread dough covered with squares of waxed paper.

We'd find ourselves standing around Nana's long table, six or seven kids, supervised by aunts. With companionable squabbling, we'd roll out sugar cookies with child-sized rolling pins that Grandpa had turned from seasoned apricot branches on his wood lathe.

Images of cookie baking remain: fireplace crackling, carols playing in a distant corner, female voices fussing when flour dusted the floor. Child-sized aprons that Nana sewed from gingham. Pans of cookies in fifteen different shapes, formed from cookie cutters she had collected over a lifetime. Homemade colored sugar, red and green. Aluminum push-tubes of buttery frosting.

We cousins enjoyed each other. We loved and respected each other's parents. Some of us shared a tighter bond than others. Sometimes the social chemistry just seemed to work.

A couple who watched our families interact during a beach trip remarked later that they couldn't tell which child belonged to which mother. My mother and aunts took their observation as a compliment.

In photographs taken at our childhood parties, we can name each guest, even fifty years later. Everyone is a cousin.

Chapter Twelve
Paying the Piper

Some cousins recall only criticism from Nana. They failed to forge a bond, a failing that was not their fault. As first-born granddaughter, I have no explanation, no excuse for Nana except that she was old when the last grandchildren came along. Her energy had been diffused by a lifetime of coping with problems. Over the years she grew fretful and short tempered. She became occupied with health problems like arthritis and gout. The tag-end grandchildren suffered.

Some of the grandchildren came as a package when Nana's youngest daughter, Mary, wed Earl Rydberg, a widower with five children. They do not recall Nana with the fondness that I do, but they enjoyed an uncommon bond with their father's mother, who helped raise them after their mother died. They were not looking for another grandmother.

Some of them thought she was cranky, but the truth is more benign. Nana possessed a relaxed, benevolent nature that she indulged on a one-to-one basis. Task oriented, forced to work hard from childhood, she looked to children to do their fair and proper share; much less than she had done at their age. When faced with five new grandchildren, she saw only the meals that needed to be cooked and the beds that needed to be made. There was never time for her to relax, to take them shopping, or to get to know them as individuals.

They came to visit with the grudging reluctance of teenagers torn away from their baseball games and their friends. Weekend visits represented two days of stress and confusion for Nana when she was in her mid-sixties. She did her best, but she forgot to give them kindness in her need to provide them food and shelter.

When Nana and Grandpa took summer road trips, they invited their biological grandchildren along. In my twelfth summer we embarked on an adventure,

Grandpa, Nana, Aunt Mary (before she married), my brother Mel, and I. We set off in a GMC pickup and camper, bound for Vancouver, British Columbia. During the two-week trip, we shared a motel room, dined together, fished and cooked our catch at river's edge. We told the truth to the Border Inspection team and watched as they tossed our peaches into the trash bin. But we understood it was the right thing to do.

My brother and I were treated as equals. We knew that we were valued. Grandpa taught us to read a compass, to query about rates and to inspect a motel room before renting it. We discussed current events over breakfast.

We watched Grandpa shave gray stubble from his aging chin, and watched Nana clean partial plates in a glass of fizzing water. We visited botanical gardens and learned to curb our impatience when we passed tourist spots more interesting to our ages, twelve and fourteen.

Following Grandpa's example, we bought maps and logged our progress every evening. We jotted travel notes in our diaries. We thrived by example. Nana and Grandpa had no need for harsh words or corrections. We saw and we copied the way that things were done.

Through the years, Nana and Grandpa managed to include all their grandchildren in their road trips. As long as they were able, they traveled to Yellowstone and Zion, across Canada and to the deserts of the Southwest. They took my mother and some of my sisters to Ohio to meet my father's parents while the rest of us worked on the farm.

Traveling with grandparents when we were at the brink of our adolescence formed lasting impressions. We observed our grandparents at the same time we were forming ideas about relationships. Theirs added a different and valuable perspective. They taught us how to grow older with grace and wisdom. At her deathbed, I remembered to tell Nana, "Thank you." Our trips with Nana and Grandpa are memories that we cousins share.

Travel was a luxury reserved for grandchildren, after land values soared and Nana began selling off her acres. My mother and her sister's memories are of a leaner time when their father struggled with a variety of jobs to supplement the farm. Grandpa never made more than three hundred dollars a month in his lifetime and Nana never held a job outside the house.

Among rural farmers, everyone lived about the same. If Grandpa and Nana lived better than most, it was only because they were industrious and frugal.

In 1936, they purchased a new car and a farm truck because the old vehicles were held together with baling wire and wouldn't make it another mile. Depression prices for manufactured goods had hit rock bottom; it was a good time to buy. To afford the purchases, Nana and Grandpa put their daughters to work on the farm and cut out all the extras. They didn't replace the vehicles until after WWII.

Through forty years of farming, Grandpa and Nana had their share of setbacks: weather, crop failures and difficulty getting hired help. One year, men drove into the apricot orchards and picked the trees clean while the family slept. An entire year's income from the crop disappeared overnight.

Grandpa's cancelled bank checks, saved in a box for nearly seventy years, give clues to their circumstances. Each month he wrote only six to eight checks. In 1926, one check was written to the grocery store in Moorpark for five dollars to pay off their monthly charge. By 1946, the monthly charge had increased to fifteen dollars. When natural gas came to the Conejo, he paid three dollars. On one occasion he paid the Borchard Brothers fifteen dollars to level a field for planting alfalfa. A few times a year, Nana ordered supplies from Sears Roebuck. Her checks to Sears Roebuck, written for fifteen dollars, were often the largest expenditure of the year.

Grandpa never borrowed from a bank. While his Norwegian neighbors borrowed to expand their citrus orchards and to purchase tractors and equipment, Grandpa maintained a strict cash policy.

In later years, Bank of A. Levy owned some of the biggest farms in the Conejo. Bank officials deemed it in their best interests to allow the farmers to remain on the land rather than foreclosing. But in many cases, farmers owed more than their land was worth. In time, escalating land values saved many a family farm from foreclosure.

Grandpa, stubborn and willful, had the satisfaction of knowing that what he owned was his. He might have taken a loan against his farm, but his father presented an insurmountable obstacle. Nils Olsen didn't trust banks. He retained his name on the deeds to his sons' lands and he refused to sign any bank loan papers. Grandpa owed his solvency to his father, who died after the Depression ended.

His 1906 Webster's Dictionary is worn and dog-eared, probably the result of his need to learn a second language from its pages. Such things are good to know about a grandfather. Many of us recall sitting beside Grandpa as he tried to teach us to count to ten in Norwegian. Like many immigrants' children, he could not write his childhood language, could only recall it from the spoken language of his memory.

He tried to teach us. Over and over we would recite *en, to, tre, fire, fem, seks, sju, åtte, ni, ti.* How hard my little brain labored to retain the strange sounds, to be able to recite them the next time Grandpa asked. But the task seemed impossible. My mother could not help. She had not learned her father's language. Perhaps Grandpa had become nostalgic in his later years and realized the value of retaining his culture. Perhaps he was too busy making a living to teach his own children. He would be pleased, I think, to know that some of his grandchildren remember.

In 1957, two brothers with Italian surnames and heavy New Jersey accents moved their families into the Conejo, and the valley began to change. They seemed wrapped in a shroud of mystery. Their children were in fifth grade with me. One of the boys told the class that his father and his uncle were helping Mr. Janss with his bookkeeping. In the next year, four thousand homes were built on the Janss Ranch.

Around the same time, Mr. Sarto, an old man who ran a bakery in the San Fernando Valley, began calling on my great-uncles. On Sunday mornings he might arrive with pastries and kitchen-table conversation about the world outside the Conejo. The great-uncles began looking forward to his visits.

He wanted to buy their farms. He wanted to become a farmer; wanted his sons to become farmers.

The great-uncles hedged and considered. In the end, they sold their land to him for the value of farmland (not as development property) and had cause to regret that they didn't wait another year. They sold for less than it was worth. Sarto's sons reaped the profits from the sale of the land.

Janss Corporation began its initial stages of development for Westlake Village. The event affected members of the family in different ways. How each person interpreted the events of the next few years depended on their feelings about change, about leaving the land, about leaving the family. Some were ready. They used the opportunity to sell their land and buy bigger farms in other areas of California. Some stayed in the area, adjusted to the influx of new neighbors and appreciated the ease afforded by the new shopping centers. Some retained their acreage in the Conejo and sold it off, bit by bit. Nana was among the latter.

Uncle Walter signed a contract to sell his walnut trees and his flatland, except for the house and a few acres. Uncle John sold some of his the following year. Uncle Fred sold a few acres. Aunt Josephine and Aunt Dorothy sold everything and moved north.

Nana kept hers for a few years, determined that her daughters should inherit as she had. Her siblings were old. They were ready to retire. The sale of their land allowed them to live out their lives in comfort and to leave their children provided for. It is the dream of every parent; they were happy that the good times allowed them to do this.

The promise of money seemed to accomplish what bad times had not. The family became embroiled in dispute. Some members wanted to hold onto land for speculation, others wanted to sell at once. The communal well was sold with the first acreage. Once the land began to be re-appraised from agriculture to development, taxes soared. Our own modest five acres were reappraised from $5,000 per acre to $50,000 per acre within a few years. Like a trim row of dominoes that had stood through three generations, once the first one fell there was no stopping the rest.

A difference of opinion erupted among the Kelleys, that had for years seemed such a slight point of dissent that family members agreed not to speak about. It hadn't seemed so important when the brushy hills grazed cattle in the spring and summer. With development of their land, the issue became paramount.

At the time of their grandfather's death, two of the girls, Josephine and Dorothy, were very young. Instead of land, they were given two thousand dollars each, the equivalent land value at the time. Their brother, Charlie never married. He wrote a will that left his share to his two sisters so they wouldn't be left out.

A few years later, the siblings re-divided the land to include the younger sisters in equal shares. At the time, Uncle Charlie intended to redo his will, leaving his portion divided among several of his nephews, but he died before it could be done. Under the terms of his will, his land was divided between his two sisters. They serendipitously ended up with a triple portion of land and money.

Some of the land amounted to brush-strewn hills, worth less than the flats. In the flush days of easy subdivisions, developers sought prime farmland. The siblings paid for surveys that would equally apportion the hills and flatland. In spite of their efforts, not everyone was happy with the division. Some of the girls had not married farmers. Those who left the Conejo in the early years had sold when land prices were lower. Some of the brothers sold their land to Mr. Sarto, whose sons sold it to developers. No matter how hard they tried, some were destined to benefit more than the others.

Children and grandchildren watched and listened to the discussions, rooting for "our team" and remained proud that everyone stayed so civil. There were misunderstandings and later, the plain talk that seems to come with old age, but the brothers and sisters remained good friends for all of their lives. Unlike the story of Joseph and his many-colored coat, there were few rifts that could not be worked out.

When development occurred, it seemed to blast the family apart with the force of a nuclear explosion. When the energy was spent, particles were flung to the far reaches of California. I was twelve when we moved from the Conejo, and I felt as though I had been reduced to pieces of sand. My family had lost that which made us strong. It was not so much the money that seemed to unsettle the family; it was the loss of a common connection. My cousins and I no longer attended the same schools. We no longer shared day-to-day appreciation of the same things. We were no longer—more or less—in the same financial straits.

Soon a golf course fronted the freeway. Housing tracts began to supplant the horse ranches and tomato fields. Nana and Grandpa packed up their farm on Olsen Road and moved to a farm in Paso Robles. Nana had considered her move to the Norwegian Colony a temporary one. She was sure that they would find themselves on other farmland within a few years. She ended up moving only once in her lifetime.

In later years, it wasn't unusual for land speculators to write letters offering outrageous prices for Nana's land. She sold off most of her holdings, an acre at a time, and shared the income with her family.

In 1964, inflated land values plummeted. The syndicate that purchased our former five-bedroom house and five acres tried to re-negotiate their purchase contract, two years after the fact.

Nana would have none of it. She received increasingly demanding letters and phone calls from their attorneys. Within the year, the five-bedroom house burned to the ground in a mysterious fire. The syndicate collected on the insurance and, within weeks, the buyers allowed the land to be repossessed.

By the late 50s, a family that had depended on itself, and counted each other as best friends, began to spread out over much of California: to the Salinas Valley, Grass Valley, Chico, and beyond. The ties that bound us were broken. So were our hearts. In the end, Sarto and his pastries cost us far more than anyone could have estimated.

Still, when development arrived in the Norwegian Colony, it did not come uninvited. When Richard Pederson retired, he married and moved to town. Wanting to see his property "used to provide youth the benefits of Christian education," he donated one hundred thirty acres to the Lutheran Church. His land was dedicated for Cal Lutheran College.

Richard's brothers, Peder and Lawrence, his sister, Anna, and the Olsen brothers, Oscar and Nicholas, were less motivated to donate their land or to sell for marginal prices. They intended to leave their land to their families. In a series of phone calls and letters, Cal Lutheran public relations men tried without success to convince the remaining farmers to add their land to the donation.

In the end, the college purchased what they needed from Richard and his sister, Anna, and built a beautiful college, Cal Lutheran. Mrs. Pederson's house was moved from its original site and earthquake-proofed. It now houses a music room for the college's music department.

The college was later renamed California Lutheran University, and stands on prime farmland at the corner of Olsen Road.

Chapter Thirteen
Making Cents of It

In 1957, Nana and Grandpa moved from their farm on the Conejo to Paso Robles. In the old European manner, Grandpa needed to provide a farm where his son could continue to work the land. Farming had to move north.

As the time for them to leave grew near, my sisters and I were gripped by a sense of loss as final as if Grandpa and Nana were leaving their homelands and moving across an ocean. We had not visited Paso Robles, but we hated even the name. We could scarcely imagine life without the house on Olsen Road.

We were conscripted to wrap Nana's treasures in tissue and newsprint. I worked with downcast eyes and a lump in my throat too big to swallow. Nana's and Grandpa's leaving felt like death. Worse than death. We were losing them and the farm at the same time.

With bittersweet longing, my brother, sister and I spent our last hours in Nana's yard. We stood in the granary and inhaled the scent of oats and mice, ran atop the rock wall, straddled the water tank like a horse, climbed the tank house steps, opened the Dutch doors of the playhouse that Grandpa had built for his daughters. We passed from one space to another, trying to absorb the sights and the smell of orange blossoms on the breeze.

Forty years later I recall it exactly as it was, for I focused all of my senses on capturing it inside me.

As if walking to our own execution, we passed among the honeybees across the clover lawn, closed our eyes and memorized the sighing of the wind in the eucalyptus trees. We filled the car with oranges and lemons.

When my mother slowly circled the car around the farmyard perimeter road and headed east, I thought my heart would break.

Today, Grandpa's mail-order farmhouse house is gone, along with the barn and most of the outbuildings. Only the trees remain. Distances seem smaller. The Oaks Shopping Mall is a half-dozen stop lights from the farm. A trip back to visit has all the elements of a class reunion, happiness and sadness rolled into one bittersweet experience.

In later years, the farm became "ours" because we still owned it in our hearts. We fumed at the audacity of the city dwellers that desecrated our land. No matter that Grandpa had transferred possession, we raged at the city boys who set fire to the eucalyptus grove and burned it nearly to the ground. We tried to understand how someone could spray paint graffiti inside the Indian caves. We felt personally violated.

Gradually the land has lost its hold on us. We have learned that memories remain pristine when held in the timeless recesses of our recollection. When we are together, my cousins agree that it is the same for them. Whenever a family reunion brings us back, it is the memories that we try to find.

Who but us knows that in the breach of a hill beyond Kelley Road, five arrowheads were found on a September morning in 1954? Who else knows that a mountain lion sunned itself in the crotch of an oak tree where we had played only minutes earlier? That a rabid skunk was cornered beneath our water tank? That an asphalt driveway covers the old mink farm? That my brother, at ten years of age, hiked from Borchard Road to the top of Old Boney after swearing my six-year-old sister to secrecy?

On our last trip to Olsen Road, my mother's face reflected her memories. She gazed at the bluffs, across the *Wuthering Heights* moors to the pepper tree that grew crooked because she had straddled it like a pony. Her eyes followed the sun setting in the west, a serendipitous *adieu* for her final visit.

Wisps of grass waved in the breeze, progeny of the seeds planted by my grandfather.

Beer bottles and campfire soot disfigured the Indian caves in the hill. My thoughts must have mirrored my mother's: *for five generations, Olsens maintained a covenant with that hill. Look what has happened. Inch by inch we have destroyed that which we loved.*

Grandpa sold some of his land to Cal Lutheran College because he would not see it developed by his own hand. It was not by accident that he returned only once before his death.

My mother bit back tears. A movement interrupted her reverie; a cottontail, hopped toward the hollow where the barn once stood. Apparently the rattlesnakes are gone as well.

The land seems broken, carved into lots that destroy the symmetry of the land. Some of the trees still stand, but the groaning of eucalyptus is lost in traffic sounds.

My mother and I agree that we are hypocrites. It is easier to blame urban sprawl than to admit that we relinquished our bond to the earth.

Modern farmers wrestle with the same question. Development is the only way that they can recoup their losses, pay off bank loans, provide for a retirement and send their children to college. They curse the city that ultimately brings high prices for land that couldn't make them a living.

An alfalfa farmer told me that in a boom year he made enough on his farming to purchase two small lots in town. He turned around and sold them within weeks. By the time escrow closed he had made more profit on their sale than he had in his twenty-six years of growing alfalfa. That is a sad story, made sadder by the fact that others have made their fortunes without knowing what alfalfa is.

Chapter Fourteen
Starting Over

On December 23, 1957, we piled into our car and drove two hundred miles north to visit Nana's new house. It was the year of the hundred year rain. We pulled over at the Rincon and waited an hour for the waves and the tide to subside. They crashed over the seawall and flooded the Pacific Coast Highway.

We discovered a pink and white striped hamburger stand in Buellton that served malts and French fries, and we established a new family tradition. At Pismo Beach we passed a gigantic rock in the middle of the highway, our halfway point. At the Cuesta Grade we found a mountain with a seven-percent grade and a harrowing view of deep ravines. In the rain, it seemed even steeper. At Paso Robles we found a quiet town with wide streets and a beautiful city park and we began to hope.

At the mailbox, "The Olsen Ranch" sign that Grandpa had formed by beating strap steel on an anvil, already hung on its welded pipe. With our first glance we were prepared to forgive Nana and Grandpa for moving.

We should have trusted them to know what a homeplace should be. The house was grand. It rose two stories over a dark, forbidding basement reached by wickedly narrow concrete steps. A huge wood-burning cook stove stood in a long back porch beside a table that could hold twenty farmhands.

The farm shop had a dirt floor that smelled of diesel just like the old one. We discovered a pair of bunkhouses, freshly swept, with tiny shower stalls. Showers were new to us. We were accustomed to claw-foot bathtubs.

We crossed a narrow footbridge that spanned a creek in flood stage and entered a dairy barn with concrete floors, redolent with an odor of stale cow manure. Sheep we were accustomed to, but the scent of cow was unfamiliar, sweet and haunting.

Nana had become friends with the farmers who sold them the place, Les and

Jenny. They seemed as connected to the farm as we were to the Conejo. Their children's names were etched in cement at the corner of the patio. We saw them at church on Sunday and Jenny's sad, Italian smile told that us all that we needed to know. It had not been by choice that they gave up the farm.

The house was old and covered with thick layers of oil-based enamel. Even the paint planned to stay. Nana's new house was designed with cubbies and built-in shelves. Arched doorways connected the rooms and a fireplace held a huge oak log. Grandpa's books and magazines already filled a pair of bookcases. In each bedroom, built-in cabinets, desks and linen closets covered an entire wall. Each second story bedroom had a view of the farm.

In the summer it would become the aunts' project to wallpaper the upper bedrooms. While the cousins played in the lawn sprinklers, my mother's sisters would gossip and put up Alberta peaches, paper and paint, rearrange furniture, and work in Nana's vegetable garden.

The barn dwarfed the out-buildings. Grandpa's hay pulley already hung above stacks of alfalfa bales in the tall, tin-roofed hay barn. The sweet, musty scent of dried alfalfa was new to us.

Instead of eucalyptus, this ranch had Valley Oaks dripping with mistletoe and Spanish moss, a reservoir for swimming, and woodlands perfect for hunting Easter eggs. Our mothers seemed equally enchanted. Months earlier, they had choked back their tears and tried to make peace with their parent's move. Now they could be happy.

It was our mothers who found the way to differentiate between the farms. The first was forever to be called "The Home Place". The second was simply, "Grandpa's farm". When Uncle Neil took over the farming, we began referring to the house as "Nana's House". We had less reason to venture out to the fields, so it ceased to be a farm and became simply the house where Nana served cookies and tea.

She and Grandpa lived out their lives in the farmhouse, shaded from the California sun by full-grown cottonwood trees. Their lives seem idyllic in today's world, but they wouldn't wish to be cloaked in a veil of nostalgia. No one would claim that they were perfect. Grandpa was especially hard on his son. He and Uncle Neil argued over Neil's agricultural college farming methods, which seemed to contradict Grandpa's own hard-won wisdom.

Stubborn and quiet, Grandpa maintained the habits of a second generation American. On reflection, he wouldn't have thought his life remarkable, only satisfying.

I think of Nana often, when the wind teases the young branches of the redwoods I planted in her honor. Not sycamores, for they are too thirsty. Not cottonwoods for they are messy, each spring exuding basketsful of cottony hairs that cover the ground and blow into the open doorway. Like the dusty blue gum eucalyptus that Lars Pederson and Nils Olsen planted for firewood, there are better varieties. The old ways have passed, but not the scrape of limb on roof. That sound is eternal.

REFLECTIONS

By the 1880s, the fertile farm valleys of California had filled with farmers. Thirty-some years after American laws stripped native-born Californios of their land grants, after the Forty-Niners moved on and the gold rush settled down, the land was ripe for farming. San Diego, Santa Barbara and San Francisco were thriving sea towns. A few men became millionaires when they built railroads with public money and cheap Chinese labor, arteries that opened up California's interior valleys to farmers.

It had been José de la Guerra's fortune to count the Rancho El Conejo among his holdings. During his stewardship, the land remained untilled. Although he was an aggressive rancher and trader, de la Guerra was no farmer. Through a series of events dictated by bankers, politicians and nature (in the form of droughts and floods) the land changed hands once, and twice, and once more again.

The arrival of determined European immigrants on the southeastern edge of Ventura County pressed plow to furrow and fields to barley and wheat. Earlier arrivals purchased the land for two to three dollars an acre from land brokers who knew a good thing when they saw it. Later arrivals like Caspar Borchard, Sr. paid a little over six dollars per acre for the same land, after bankers and drought wore the edges from the original pioneers.

It was a time of cheap land, of horse and men power where each depended on the other. It was a time where life expectancy was low, owing to accidents and illnesses. Family histories record children dying from a cold caught while swimming on a cool day, from a lion's mauling and from tuberculosis. My grandfather was one of three children in his family to live to adulthood when seven others died in childhood. Is it any wonder that family photographs show mothers

121

solemn faced and stoic, fathers worn and bent? People just plain wore out.

The pragmatism that created a rural network in the Conejo Valley differed little from that of other areas. More than simply the story of the Conejo, this is the story of a thousand valleys.

I was born at the end of an era. I watched my vast, extended family fuss and rally, celebrate and render mutual aid. I never questioned that my world-view was normal and reasonable. Nor do I now. But by every standard that I apply, it seems as though society has lost more than it has gained in the second part of the twentieth century.

Communities hold parades and build museums and interpretive centers. We don pioneer garb and give spinning and churning demonstrations to school children, but we are reenacting a memory. For the most part, the pragmatism and grit of America is gone, and we are only pretending when we say that it is not.

So what remains? Is it only our memories and those twists in the loops of our DNA, those odd ways of thinking and behaving that set us apart from the rest of society as the last generation of farm children turned urban? Some of us have trouble fitting into a culture where polished and poised are the new hallmarks, where plain speech and bull-headedness create social discord. Still too close to the old ways, we see little reason to trade our values for others that seem artificially slick and calculated. We accept progress with a sigh, pick and choose what we will embrace.

We are the last generation to be reared under the expectation that hard work will be rewarded. We have watched men without calluses become millionaires in an electronic age and we feel betrayed.

We are the men and women raising sheep and cattle on our five-acre suburban plots while we work full time jobs in town. We grow peaches and apples and spend our weekends canning them into Mason jars before returning to our town jobs. We can't understand why our children won't help in the family garden, why our children and grandchildren have rejected our belief in hard work and have replaced it with confidence in a New World Economy. Our advice, our spirituality, our way of life seems to have become archaic. We are becoming a service economy where no one wants to be the servant.

Our children think we are dinosaurs, fools for our work ethic and our slavish devotion to the old ways, and maybe we are. We seem to be caught in a schizophrenic blur between the old and the new.

We distrust bio-engineered food and altered milk. We remember when things tasted real. Many of us can still milk a cow. We recall our grandmother's roses and geraniums. We know that the nursery industry has hybridized nature until the scent of flowers has disappeared along with their ability to weather climate changes. We recall when trees were planted in both male and female varieties, the females making a mess in the yards with their pods and debris. But they attracted the pollen that now floats uselessly in the air. Now we sneeze, and take our allergy medicine, medicate our children's asthma. But we remember that the old days were healthier.

We study the photographs of our ancestors and we notice that hardly anyone was fat. We remember the Fifties, when sodas, flavored drink mixes, white bread and potato chips came into our diets, when sugar became synonymous with a mother's love. We remember school prayer, spankings, being sent outside to play, having to change into play clothes. We remember twice a week baths, and saying 'thank you', and calling our parent's friends by Mister and Missus instead of by their first names.

Now we are hounded by the guilt of our abandonment. Things are out of kilter and we suspect that we are to blame. Our grandparents' photographs remind us that we forgot their lessons along the way. They were disciplined in a way that we are not, focused in a way that we have lost.

True, theirs was a world of fewer choices. I doubt, given the diversity of our temptations, that they would have done any better than we have. But the fact is, we failed to heed their maxim: Waste not, want not. Now we must brace ourselves for the consequences.

We are tied to the thinking that formed our values. From a farmer's viewpoint, when a man moves away from his farm and takes a job in town, he feels trapped. He has lost his stillness. The baying of a neighbor's dog or the screeching of tires becomes almost unbearable cacophony. The city puts off unnatural heat that emanates from the concrete, from steam vents and even from the crush of human bodies.

Skyscrapers create unnatural canyons closed to cooling breezes. Like a wildfire, the city creates its own climate, rank with stench. Air-borne particles cling to the skin and suffocate the pores. The water tastes metallic, and of chlorine. It runs warm from the tap, not chilled from the recesses of the earth.

Sometimes I consider how far my cousins and I have deviated from our great-grandmother's view. We daughters of the soil seem to spring from our roots in different manner. Some of us flock to town and thrive, don high heels and long, lacquered nails and take jobs as secretaries. Others see themselves as partners with husbands or brothers in a long tradition of the West. This being the case, we drive a pick-up truck and a tractor with equal enthusiasm, count a new pair of Wranglers as our spring wardrobe and greet any man as a friend and peer.

Yet, we seem caught in the middle, unsure where we belong. We work at town jobs but drive a tractor on Saturday mornings. We daydream of satin robes and vacations to faraway places. We help castrate sheep, but wear gloves to protect our nail polish. Some of us marry city boys and spend our lives trying to figure out why some things make us so cantankerous.

Is the farmer's view a romantic one? Undoubtedly. Is it fair? Maybe not. Maybe the issue of fairness is beside the point. Like nationalism or patriotism, we agrarians cling to a set of values that defines our being.

One of the benefits of living in a family enclave was the opportunity to observe our kin. When a child watches his grandfather experiment with crop rotation and animal husbandry, when a child observes his father's wisdom and watches him solve problems, he learns the lessons for a lifetime.

Schoolbooks would have us believe that there are no social lines, just as there are no racial lines, but we know better. Since peasants began clustering crofts together to create towns, since sea trade and specialization necessitated a cash economy, we have had a farmer class. Rita Mae Brown, in her book *Starting From Scratch* penned it well: for the English speaking, the situation was made serious in 1066 when Harold fell at Hastings, shot through the eye with an arrow. Since the Normans overwhelmed the Anglo-Saxons and hybridized our language with French we have had 'farmer English' and 'city English', called in its proper form 'high' English and 'low' English. High English is Latinesque, grand and expressive. We use it to describe culture and enjoyment of life.

If a Norman nobleman sat to dine, it was on beef. The farmer/serf raised oxen. Deer served at table was venison. Lords dined on pork, farmers raised pigs, the same for fowl and chicken, and the list continues. Farmers kept their language where they died, helped, dressed, worked, and were happy. Should someone wish to gain acceptance into urban or court society, they replaced these simple words with perish, aided, clothed, toiled and experienced felicity.

The farmer continued to use the low form and was often thought a dullard when judged next to his city cousin. Those of us who knew our farmer grandparents realize that this was not so. When the noblest of Lords falls into a swill he will surely holler "Help!" not "Aid!" Aid seldom really helps.

To watch a farmer build a tractor part on his lathe or repair a broken implement is to watch an engineer at work. To sit around a table and hear farmers argue politics, economics and social policy is to attend a grass roots university. The lessons go on, day and night, for those of us who are listening.

Economic factors may be conspiring against the family farmer; a cash economy may favor the urbanites, but the farmer should feel no shame. Although the farmer might envy the coins jingling in the pockets of his city brother, the farmer does not begrudge him. Rather he is frustrated because mega-dollars, not brawn or stubbornness, now define success.

In the early days of farming, ownership of land defined a man's worth. A man with many sons and daughters, much land and many horses, had little need of cash except to buy staples and to pay his taxes. His grain seed was hearty. He could save a portion in reserve to plant in the spring. The land was verdant and fertile. Fertilizers and sprays were not needed. Horsepower was simply that, cheaply fed on hay and grain that the farmer grew.

When tractors arrived, the farmer fared even better. Eggs and butter paid for his staples, flour sacks provided cloth for his children's garments until they started school. Women and girls grew cash crops in their gardens and sewed the family's clothing.

Careful stewardship is synonymous with farming, an image both wholesome and heartening, even if it isn't always true. As farmers, we believe in the concept even when we travel to the city to buy clothing and canned peaches. Like everyone else, we believe that our countrymen can rest easy, knowing that the farmer is upholding the tenets that made America great.

WWII brought mass consumerism and, with it, an end to institutionalized frugality. Farmers left the farm and learned that impulse was a lot more fun than saving for a rainy day. Television brought a world of consumer goods and places to visit. Farmers learned that they liked to travel. Increasingly, they lacked the cash to indulge in their wants and needs while public money favored the emerging classes of landless poor. Farmers found that they couldn't compete in a cash economy and they couldn't qualify for assistance, even if they wanted to.

When the farmer's children clamored to attend college, they discovered that even land-poor farmers owned too many assets for their children to qualify for grants or scholarships. Applications had to be turned in by January 31, too early for farmers to compute their expenses of the previous year. Under existing rules, their children didn't qualify for government money.

Everywhere we turned, society counted on the farmer to feed the nation and the world cheaply, while others made their fortunes selling goods and services that raised the farmer's cost of doing business. By 1959, the cycle caught up with us. Victor Davis Hanson, in his book, *The Land Was Everything*, writes that decades ago, a twenty pound box of plums sold for $4. Today it still sells for $4 while production costs have skyrocketed. The shopper takes them home from the supermarket for $1.99 a pound.

For the small farmer, the ensuing decades have intensified the gulf. Worse yet, the farmer's income arrives in seasonal increments, much of it in mid or late summer, while his expenses continue year round. Instead of dancing all night at a harvest celebration like his great-grandfathers, the modern farmer is more likely to sit at the kitchen table with his wife and juggle unpaid bills.

A similar gulf divides stockman and farmer. Stockmen raise cattle and horses, trusting on the rains to keep the ravines and canyons fortified with nourishing grass. Many of them feel like the farmer is crazy to struggle against nature. Why, they ask, put all that work into breaking the ground? Why not sit back and let cattle do what they do best: eat? In contrast, the farmer values his own physical labor. He often considers the stockman lazy.

I understand the argument both ways.

A stockman cousin remarked to me once at a family gathering how hard my father had worked us on the farm. I found myself wanting to respond, "What else were we supposed to do with our time?" but I held my tongue. Intellectually, I knew the answer. I have been to Paris, to college, and have found pleasure in a number of avocations, but for a moment my core beliefs clamored to be heard.

To a farmer, hard, physical work is so fine a discipline, leaves a body so sated at the end of a day, that the ache of a day's labor is the feeling of being alive. Even when forced to quit my high school tennis team because I was needed in the fields after school, I understood my father's reasoning. My disappointment was a tradeoff. My value to my family was a matter of survival. To a kid, that's a pretty heady feeling.

The enmity between farmer and city dweller has been stoked by the consumerism that convinces us that we need all things, regardless of our ability to pay for them. The farm wife is characterized as thrifty, comfortable in a worn-out dress without a blush of self-consciousness. This isn't true, probably never was.

The truth is that a farmer's wife doesn't indulge herself in recreational shopping trips to the Mall. She doesn't allow herself to visit Macy's until the last week of their seasonal sale and then she justifies her purchases as lay-away birthday gifts. Sometimes, the homemade jams and butter-light cinnamon rolls that she gives for Christmas may seem a little provincial, even to her.

So the farmer continues to farm with one eye on the encroaching city. By the time it arrives he has experienced the accompanying rise in property taxes, has fended off a half-dozen realtors and knows, to the penny, what his land is worth.

The irony is not lost on most farmers. They face complicated formulas of how to sell. Some of their sons want to remain on the land. Some do not. They keep an eye on inheritance tax laws and calculate their net worth. They tally the costs of retirement trips against sitting out their last days on the Home Place, trying to stay out of their children's hair.

They secretly hope that some developer will offer them big bucks for their property and they can sell for many times the land's value while their neighbors continue to farm and maintain the rural atmosphere. It is not only Los Angelenos fleeing to a retirement paradise that want to close the gate behind them. The farmer is often guilty of the same.

This is the reality of farming in California today. This was the case in the Conejo Valley of 1957 when development exploded with the intensity of a bomb. Within a couple of years it seemed as though the entire valley floor had been covered in houses, streets and blacktop.

Joe Russell, Sr., a pioneer son whose father established the Russell Ranch (part of which is now Westlake Village), wrote his impressions of the valley into two volumes, *Cattle on the Conejo* and, later, *Heads and Tails...and Odds and Ends*. He said it for all of us in his understatement; "Those of us who have lived in El Conejo and Ventura County all our lives are a little surprised, and even a little bewildered, at what has happened to us in the space of a few short years."

As a wave of newcomers entered the floodgates to initiate a new era, another gate opened at the other end of the valley by which the farmers and ranchers quietly left.

◆BRANCHES

BORCHARD FAMILY (Arrived in the Conejo in 1887)
- ◆ Caspar Borchard, Sr. (purchased farms in the Conejo Santa Ana and Texas)
- ◆ Wife: Theresa Maning Borchard (died at 49 of stomach cancer)
  - ◆ Caspar and Theresa Borchard's Children:
  - ◆ Mary (raised her siblings after her mother's death, remained a spinster)
  - ◆ **Rosa** (my great-grandmother. Married Silas Kelley.)
  - ◆ Caspar, Jr. (Farmed in the Conejo. Carved up the oak table.)
  - ◆ Teresa (After her husband's death, her sons formed the Borchard Brothers Ranch in partnership with her. Married cousin Edward.)
    - ◆ Teresa and Edward's Children
      - ◆ Edward
      - ◆ Robert
      - ◆ Allen
  - ◆ Frank (farmed in Santa Ana)
  - ◆ Charles (farmed in Santa Ana)
  - ◆ Leo (farmed in Santa Ana)

  - ◆ Caspar's Relatives:
    - ◆ Brother, John (purchased Caspar's farm when he was delayed in Germany for four years.)
    - ◆ Brother, Christian (original family member to come to California. Herded sheep in Antioch upon his arrival.)
    - ◆ Cousins, Freidrichs' (farmed opposite side of Newbury Park)

KELLEY FAMILY (Arrived in the Conejo in 1889)
- ◆ John Reily Kelley (Widower who traveled by wagon train from Nebraska. Known for riding a huge black stallion.)
  - ◆John's Children:

- John Reily, Jr. (traveled three times back and forth from Texas and Oklahoma by wagon train trying to make a living. Had 10 children. His wife was Aunt Lucy.)
- **Silas** (My great-grandfather. Married Rosa Borchard.)
  - Silas and Rosa's Children:
    - Charlie (A bachelor. Lived with his widowed mother until his death of a heart attack at 49.)
    - **Theresa** (My grandmother. Married Oscar Olsen.)
    - John: (Married Babe.)
      - John and Babe's Children:
        - Johnny (Married to Alta. Became partially paralyzed)
        - Catherine (Retired international educator, married to an oil company executive, John Moragne.)
        - Michael (Married to fellow Veterinarian, Merrie. Owns their own practice at Cottage Hospital in Oxnard.)
- Walter:(Married to Helga. No children. Kept a dairy. Later raised walnuts in the Conejo.)
- Fred: (Married to Mildred. He was Fire Chief at Hueneme.)
  - Fred's Children:
    - Fred Jr. (Retired space engineer. Lives on original Kelley property.)
    - Billy (Remains in the Conejo.)
    - Patricia. (Lives in Arroyo Grande.)
- Rose: (Married to Harry Fletcher until she died of breast cancer at 36.)
  - Rose's Children:
    - Ralph (Lives in Grass Valley)
    - Donnie (Killed by a panther at the Lion Farm when he was almost three.)
    - Patrick (A baby when she died.)
- Dorothy (Married Earl Ashby. Ran a beauty shop in the Lion Farm. Died of cancer.) Children: Juney and Jill.
- Josephine (Married Cyril Colwell. Both worked at the State Hospital until retirement.
  - Josephine's Children:
    - Donna (Lives in South Lake Tahoe)

- ◆ Jackie (Lives in South Lake Tahoe)
- ◆ Vickie (Lives in Nipomo)
- ◆ Silas Kelley's sisters
  - ◆ Aunt Lizzy (Abandoned by her husband, a Texas cowhand. She was ranch cook for the Caspar Borchard, Jr. Ranch until her 60s.)
  - ◆ Aunt Minny (Lived in Texas, came out to visit every two years. Wore cast-off, formal black taffeta dresses regardless of the weather.)

OLSEN FAMILY (Arrived in Conejo in 1887)
- ◆ Nils Olsen: born Nils Uren. Immigration renamed him Olsen because his father's name was Ole. (Ole's son or Olsen.)
- ◆ Ellen Fjorstad Olsen (Fjorstad was changed to Iverson by Immigration. Died at 53.)
  - ◆ Nils and Ellen's Children:
    - ◆ Ludwig (Married Hazel. No children. Farmed alongside Oscar until he moved to Santa Barbara.)
    - ◆ **Oscar** (My grandfather. Married Theresa Kelley.)
      - ◆ **Oscar and Theresa's** Children:
        - ◆ Arthelia Honerkamp (Husband Alloys (Jack). Moved to Whittier in 1956.
          - ◆ Arthelia's Children: Larry, Helen, Vincent, Rosemary.)
        - ◆ **Eugenia (Jean) Thompson** (My mother. Married Wilbur Thompson. Moved to Shandon in 1959.)
          - ◆ Thompson Children: Mel, Teresa Anne, Martha, Joan, Matthew Paul, Brian and Laura.
        - ◆ Mary Lois Rydberg (Husband, Earl. Lives in Oxnard.)
          - ◆ Mary's Children: Frank, Daniel, Roseanna, Kathleen and James. Stepchildren: Suzanne, Pete, Jeff, Gail and Sharon.
        - ◆ Neil Olsen (Married Gisela Fritschle. Lives on his farm in Paso Robles.
          - ◆ Children: Bernard, Ingrid and Eric.
    - ◆ Nicholas (Married Sarah. Remained on the Norwegian Colony until his death. Built the miniature stagecoach that is displayed at the Stagecoach Inn.)

- Nicholas' Children:
  - Gerald (Gerry), retired Information Officer for Ventura City College. Active in Community Affairs.
  - Jeanette (Lives in Redding, CA)
  - Jeannie (Lives in Thousand Oaks)
  - David. (Lives in Thousand Oaks)
- Paula, Nora, Emma, Nora, Laura, Ned and Thora (Nils' and Ellen's children who died in childhood.)

THE NORWEGIAN COLONY:

- Ole Anderson (Farmed Lot #1, never married. Died of typhus. His land was later bought by Nils Olsen and became Grandpa's and Nana's Farm.)
- Lars and Karen Pederson (Farmed Lot #2. He died of typhus. Karen and her sons, Rich, Lawrence and Pete returned to the Conejo in the mid-1910s and farmed until their retirement. Some of their land was donated to Cal Lutheran University.)
- Ole Nilson (Farmed Lot #3. Nil's cousin. Moved to Northern California in a drought year.)
- George and Lina Hanson. (Farmed Lot #4. He died of typhus. She and her daughter returned to Norway.)
- Nils Olsen (Farmed Lot #5. Remained on the Norwegian Colony until his retirement. His sons' families still own part of the original land.)

Anne Schroeder

ABOUT THE AUTHOR

A fifth generation Californian, Anne Schroeder's love of the West is fueled by stories of bandits and hangings, of her great-great grandfather and his neighbors working together to blast the Norwegian Grade out of solid rock, of Indian caves, of women who made their own way.

Schroeder writes about what she knows, the history and locale of the Far West. Her writing honors the role that women played in western expansion. She writes women's historical fiction. She is working on her fourth novel.

She worked her way through California Polytechnic State University in San Luis Obispo with a variety of odd-jobs that included waitressing at a truck-stop cafe in Cholame (where James Dean died), driving a hay truck in the summer, and working at an NBC affiliate television station.

Schroeder lives in Atascadero, California, where she uses her gasoline powered 1933 Maytag washing machine, turns homemade ice cream with a hit-and-miss engine from the turn of the century and makes costumed presentations of historical Western women for elementary school children. Luckily, her family shares her passion for old ruins and out-of-the-way places.

Author of over twenty short stories and essays published in the U.S. and Canada,(including *Potpourri, Liguorian, Skipping Stones, Lynx Eye, Western Digest, Romantic Hearts, Radiance,* and *Christian Reader*), she is currently editing a collection of short stories and poetry from promising new writers of the Pacific Northwest titled *Scent of Cedars* for Russell Dean & Company, Publishers. Her family memoir, *Branches of the Conejo: Leaving the Soil After Five Generations* recently won first place for first person/non-fiction in the William Sayoran Writing Contest.

Schroeder teaches creative writing through her local community college, owns a small pizzeria in Paso Robles, patronizes her local independent book-stores and subscribes to three small press publications each year.